More

LITTLE VISITS WITH GOD

More

LITTLE VISITS

Devotions for Families

Publishing House
St. Louis

WITH GOD

with Young Children

By ALLAN HART JAHSMANN

and MARTIN P. SIMON

Illustrations by FRANCES HOOK

Concordia Publishing House, St. Louis, Mo. 63118

© Concordia Publishing House 1961

Library of Congress Catalog Card No. 61-11549

VH 1078

Manufactured in the United States of America

Foreword

Our child Judy loves *Little Visits with God* and reads her own choices from the book regularly. No single volume has meant as much to our family life as this one.

I have carried the book to Sunday school association meetings, and I have seen eyes light up at the mention of it. My wife has used *Little Visits* to open the day at our church's vacation Bible school. And the children there were glad to listen.

Our own personal experience with these devotions has been multiplied thousands of times in Christian homes throughout our land. The widespread reception given the first volume of this type of material is largely due to the word-of-mouth advertising of grateful readers.

The authors wanted to produce a book which would bring our children (and all of us, I hope, have a lot of child in us) into a face-to-face encounter with the Gospel of Jesus Christ. That they succeeded in doing this with the first *Little Visits* is unquestionable.

The same can be said for this second heart-warming book, and more! Through it all our children will grow happier and stronger in the sunshine of God's love.

WALTER RIESS

Contents

God is a Spirit. John 4:24

Why Terry Couldn't See God

Ruth invited her little friend Terry to come to church with her. "It's God's house," said Ruth. "God talks to us there."

So Terry went to church with Ruth. On the way home Ruth said, "Terry, how did you like being in church?"

"I liked it okay," said Terry, "but where was God? I never saw Him there."

Ruth said, "Oh, He was there all the time. But nobody can see God. He isn't like us."

"Why can't we see Him?" asked Terry. "If we can't see Him, how do we know He's there?"

"Can you see the wind?" asked Ruth's mother, who was walking along and listening.

"No," said Terry.

"Then how do you know there's a wind?"

"I can see what the wind does in the trees. And I can feel it in my face," said Terry.

"Well," said Ruth's mother, "God is a Spirit. He has no body. But we can see what He does. And we can feel Him when we love Him in our heart. And we can hear Him speak when we listen to His Word."

"I guess you have to go to church awhile before you can see God that way," said Terry.

"You don't even have to go to church to see God that way," said Ruth. "You can love Him anywhere. But going to church helps you know Him because you learn about Him there."

Questions to talk about: What did Ruth call the church? Why did she call it God's house? What did Terry say on the way home? Why didn't Terry see God? In what ways is the wind like God? Can you say the Bible verse?

Bible reading for grownups: John 4:19-24.

Our prayer: Dear God, our Father in heaven, we are glad that You are a Spirit so You can be in all places, also in our church, in our homes, and in our hearts. Please live with us in *our* hearts and home, too, through Jesus Christ, our Lord. Amen.

I think about God's Word
all day long. Psalm 119:97

What's in Your Bible?

"Most people don't know what's in the Bible," said the minister on his visit to the Kay home.

"I know what's in the Bible," said little Karen Kay.

"You do?" asked the pastor. "Tell me, Karen, what's in the Bible?"

So Karen told him: "Mommie's ticket for a turkey, and one of my baby curls, and a dried-up flower is in it."

2

Do you think Karen knew what is in the Bible? No, she only knew some THINGS that were in her *mother's* Bible. But she didn't know that God's Word is in the Bible and that the way to life with God is in the Bible.

We can't find out what's in the Bible just by having the book and putting things into it. God's Word has to be learned, and a person has to think about what it says.

Long ago a man who loved God said, "I think about God's Word all day long." Do we think about what God has told us in the Bible every day — all day long — at different times of the day?

To be able to think about God's Word by ourselves, we have to know what it says. That's why we need to read and study the Bible and think about God's Word every day. Memorizing parts of the Bible helps us to think about God's Word.

A child too small to read can have somebody tell him a Bible story every day. He can also have someone teach him a Bible verse. Children who can read easy words, but not yet the Bible, can read a Bible story book or a children's devotion book, and can think about it.

As soon as a person can read the Bible by himself, he ought to do it every day. Those who do so learn to know what's in the Bible. They learn that God hates and punishes sin. They learn that Jesus is their Savior. They learn how they can have God's love. They learn how to live with God as His children.

Such things are worth thinking about very often every day.

Questions to talk about: What did Karen say was in the Bible? What did the minister mean when he said, "Most people don't know what's in the Bible"? How can even little children find out what's in the Bible? What have you

3

learned to know from the Bible? Why is it good to think about God's Word all day long?

Bible reading: Psalm 119:97-105.

Our prayer: Forgive us, heavenly Father, for knowing so little about what You have told us in the Bible. Teach us to be daily Bible readers, and give us the Holy Spirit so that we will gladly think about Your Word all day long every day. We ask this in Jesus' name. Amen.

If God is for us, who can be against us? Romans 8:31

God on Our Side

"You can't go along to the picnic," said Tom to his youngest sister. "You're too little. You'll have to stay at home." He was teasing her.

His little sister started to cry. Then she ran to her father. "Tom says I'm too little to go to the picnic," she sobbed.

"Well, you tell Tom he can't decide who goes along and who doesn't. I decide, and I want you to go," said her father.

Now the little girl was all smiles again. She didn't care

if Tom was against her. Her father was for her. "Daddy's on my side, and he said I could go, and you can't stop me," the little girl told her big brother.

In telling about God, our Father in heaven, the apostle Paul said some words almost like those of the little girl. He said, "If God is for us, who can be against us?"

Sometimes people are against us. They don't love us and may even try to harm us. And worse than that, the devil is against us. He reminds God of all the sins we have done. He wants us to be unhappy and to suffer in hell.

But Jesus died for us. Jesus paid for all our sins. That's why the Bible says, "He who did not spare His own Son, but gave Him up for us all, will He not with Him also gladly give us all other things?"

If God loves us so much that He gave up His only Son's life, then He is for us. And if God is for us, who can be against us? Nobody, not even the devil. We can say, "Go away, devil. Jesus paid for my sins. You can't say that I won't get into heaven."

That's why Paul also wrote, "Nothing will be able to separate us from the love of God in Christ Jesus, our Lord."

Let's talk about this: Why did the little girl cry? What made her smile? Who is against us? Why can we be sure that God is for us? What is the answer to the question "If God is for us, who can be against us?" Where will all who belong to Jesus get to go even if the devil says they can't?

Bible reading for older children and grownups: Romans 8:31-39.

We bow to pray: Dear Jesus, we love You for what You did for us. Because You died for us, God is on our side. If God is for us, who can be against us? Help us to believe that nothing can separate us from the love of God which we can have from You. Keep us happy in Your love, no matter what may happen to us. Amen.

*Find your joy in the Lord, and He will give you
what your heart wants.* Psalm 37:4

How to Be Happy

"I never get what I want," said Henry.

"I know how to change that," said his brother George.
"Start wanting what you get!"

At first Henry thought George was just making fun of
him. But then he said, "Maybe the things I get are what
God wants me to have. Maybe it wouldn't be good to get
everything I want. Maybe if I would pray or work hard,
God would give me what I want."

George said, "I know a Bible verse that tells you how
to get what you want." He went over to the table where
the Bible was and showed Henry Psalm 37. It said: "Find
your joy in the Lord, and He will give you what your heart
wants."

We can learn to like almost anything. Some people like
olives, others don't. Some like company, others would rather
be alone. Some like to read, others would rather play ball
or go fishing.

We usually like what we have learned to like. So why
don't we learn to like what God likes? That's the way to
become satisfied and happy. For when we love God and
the things He likes, we can be sure that He will give us
what we want.

But how can we love God and what He wants us to
enjoy? By learning to know how good He is and how much
He loved us in sending Jesus to save us. "We love Him because He first loved us."

Let's talk about this: Why did Henry complain a lot?
What did his brother George tell him? When does the Lord

6

give us what we want? What are some of the things we can be sure God wants us to have? How can we learn to love the Lord and what He wants?

Bible reading for grownups: Psalm 37:1-9.

Our prayer: Dear Father in heaven, please give us the Holy Spirit so that we will enjoy being followers of Jesus, our Savior. Help us to love what You love, so that we will always be happy, as You have promised. Amen.

I will be sorry for my sin. Psalm 38:18

Not Easy, but Right

"Okay, I admit I shouldn't have done it," said Grace. She had spoiled Dale's picture, and her father was making her tell Dale she was sorry. But Grace didn't want to.

"That's not being sorry," said Dale.

"I said I shouldn't have done it, and that's all I'm going to say," Grace snapped.

"Well," said their father, "God wants us to admit our sins, but just saying 'I did wrong' isn't enough. He also wants us to be sorry."

"All right then, I'm sorry," said Grace, feeling meaner than ever. "What else do you want me to say?"

Her father was sad that Grace felt the way she did. "It's not just the words that count," he said. "Once there was a man who kissed Jesus, and even that was a sin. Do you remember who it was?"

"Judas," said Grace, still pouting.

"Yes, Judas didn't really mean his kiss, because he didn't love Jesus," said her father. "Don't you see? It makes a dif-

7

ference *why* you do a thing or *why* you say what you say. A kiss isn't a kiss if no love goes along with it."

"No," said Dale; "and saying 'I'm sorry' isn't worth anything either if there is no being sorry along with it."

For a minute everybody was quiet. Then Grace said, "I'm sorry I spoiled your picture, Dale. You may have mine instead."

"I don't need yours, Grace. But I'm glad you're really sorry now," said Dale.

It isn't always easy to say "I'm sorry," and it's even harder to *be* sorry. But God wants us to be sorry for whatever we do wrong. When we are, He is willing to forgive us for Jesus' sake. That's plenty of reason for admitting our sins and being sorry about them.

Some questions: What had Grace done? What did she say? Why didn't Dale like what she said? Why wasn't the kiss of Judas really a kiss? Why isn't it enough just to say "I'm sorry"? What good reasons do we have for being sorry about our sins?

The Bible story about a boy who was sorry: Luke 15:11-24.

Let's talk to God: O Lord, please make us willing to admit our sins to You and to those whom we have hurt. Most of all, help us to *be* sorry for our sins, and please forgive all our sins for the sake of Jesus, our Savior, who died to pay for them. Amen.

Oh, give thanks to the Lord, for He is good;
His love lasts forever. Psalm 118:1

Something That Lasts and Lasts

"That's the third time those boys ran over my flowers," said Mrs. Ranter. "That's just enough. I'm not going to let them play in my yard any more."

So she put a lock on the gate of her yard, and the children couldn't play there any more. They were sorry, because she had swings and a slide for her grandchildren.

One day two of the boys came and said, "If we promise to be real careful about your flowers, will you let us play in your yard?"

"No," said the woman, "you had your chance. I told you twice to keep off the flowers." And she didn't open the gate.

We can be glad that God isn't like Mrs. Ranter. When we come to God and say we're sorry for what we've done wrong, does God ever close the gate? No, God always forgives for Jesus' sake. He always wants us near Him.

The Bible says, "God's love lasts forever." It never wears out; it never ends. That's something to be glad about. So we say the psalm verse, "Oh, give thanks to the Lord, for He is good. His love lasts forever."

Let's talk about this: What made Mrs. Ranter angry? Why wasn't she willing to forgive the boys? How long does God's love last? If we say to God, "Please forgive us," will He do it? Will He do it if He already has done it a hundred times? Why is God always willing to love us? What does the Bible verse tell us to do?

Bible reading for grownups: Psalm 117.

Let us bow in prayer: For Your love that never ends, we thank You, dear Father in heaven. Please help us to live like people who love You. Give us the Holy Spirit so that we will always be kind and good to others, for Jesus' sake. Amen.

*The Lord opens the eyes
of the blind.* Psalm 146:8

Learning to See Jesus' Way

Mary Jane was talking to a blind man. The blind man was telling her about some of the things he did and places where he liked to go.

"How can you do so many things when you can't see?" she asked.

The blind man reached down and patted his dog. "My dog sees for me," he said. You could hear how he felt about his dog in the way he said it.

It's wonderful that seeing-eye dogs can be trained to help blind people. The dogs use their eyes for those who cannot see. They lead the blind safely across dangerous streets and wherever they want to go.

10

Jesus often said that some people have eyes but cannot see. He meant they cannot see that they sin. They cannot see that their life is dark. They cannot see the way to heaven. They cannot see the way God wants them to live.

But those who let Jesus lead them get His eyes. He shows us that we sin. He saves us and takes us on the way to heaven. He helps us see what God wants us to do. The Bible says, "The Lord opens the eyes of the blind."

We can help the people who cannot see God and His love even though they have good eyes. We can show them that Jesus is their Savior. When they begin to see that, then they see that God loves them. Then they see a lot of other wonderful things, too. They see God's ways through the eyes of Jesus. His eyes become their eyes.

And how well do *we* see God and His ways? The Lord will also open *our* eyes if we will let Him lead us. That's why we need to pray, "Open our eyes."

Lets talk about this: What did Mary Jane ask the blind man? What did he tell her? What does a seeing-eye dog do for his master? In what way are many people blind even when they can see? What does Jesus help us to see? How can we help people to see that God loves them? Why do we need to ask the Lord to open our eyes?

Bible reading: Acts 26:14-18.

Let us pray: Dear Jesus, please open our eyes and keep them open so that we will not be blind about our sins and God's wonderful love. Help us also to show others that You are their Lord and Savior. Make us all glad to follow You, for we know that You will lead us on the way to heaven. Amen.

God made the stars also. Genesis 1:16

In the Middle of God's World

Tommy and his sister Ann sat watching the stars. The papers had said there would be a pretty show of northern lights in the sky that evening.

"You can point to any star," said Tommy, "and it's millions and millions of miles away."

"They must be awfully big, or we couldn't see them," said Ann.

"So big we can't even think how big," said Tommy.

"You know how big an atom is?" asked Ann. "There are millions of them in one little thimble, that's how small they are," she said. She had heard this in science class.

"That's funny," said Tom.

"What's funny?" asked Ann.

"I don't mean funny. I mean, well, *wonderful,* I guess. When you think of the world, you begin to understand how great God is," said Tom.

"You mean because He made both the atoms and the stars?" asked Ann.

"Both at the same time," said Tom. "Stars so very, very big that we can't even imagine how big they are. And atoms so very, very small that we can't even imagine how small they are."

"You know what?" said Ann after thinking a while. "We're in the middle between the great big things and the very little things God has made," said Ann. Then they both just sat and looked and thought some more. But it was like praying.

Questions to talk about: How far away are the stars? How big is an atom? What did Tom think was most wonderful about it all? Can you tell the Bible story of how the world was made? Where do we find this story in the Bible?

Bible reading: Genesis 1:14-19.

Let us pray: O Great and Mighty God, Maker of the stars, we see how small we are when we think of the great wonders You have made. We wonder why You care about us. But we are glad that You love us and have adopted us as Your children. Forgive us our sins for Jesus' sake, and make Your love shine in our lives. In Jesus' name we pray this. Amen.

Let him that stole
  steal no more. Ephesians 4:28

Finders Keepers?

On the way to school one day Billy saw something that looked like a baseball under a bush in front of a house. When he crawled under the bush, he saw it *was* a baseball. He was glad.

"Finders keepers," he said, and took the ball along to school. He knew that it probably belonged to the little boy who lived in the house where he found the ball, but he didn't care. He wanted the ball.

That evening Billy went home from school down an alley. Halfway home a little dog barked at him. "Why, that's Rover," said Billy. It was the dog he had gotten for his birthday. He thought the dog had run away, but there he was wiggling all over. Somebody had tied him up, so Billy petted him and started to untie him.

"Get away from my dog," said the big boy. "I found him. Beat it or I'll punch you in the nose."

Billy ran home crying. Now he didn't think "finders keepers" was a good rule. He was sorry he ever thought so. He even asked Jesus to forgive him for taking the ball.

When Billy passed the house where he had found the ball, he saw a boy in the yard, so he stopped. "Is this yours?" he asked the boy. He knew now that Jesus wanted him to return it.

"Yeah," said the boy. "Where'd you find it?"

"Never mind," said Billy, and tossed the ball to him. Then he walked on home, muttering to himself.

A little farther down the alley he heard a dog yelping behind him. It was Rover. Part of a rope was hanging from his neck.

"Rover!" said Billy, hugging and petting his dog, "you tore yourself loose to come back to me. 'Finders keepers' is sure an awful rule. Now I know why Jesus doesn't want us to steal."

Questions to talk about: What did Billy find on the way to school one day? What did he say to himself as he kept the ball? What happened on the way home? Who said "finders keepers" this time? How did Billy show that he no longer believed the rule? What does God say about stealing? What is our main reason for not stealing?

14

Bible reading for older children and adults: Ephesians 4:25-30.

Let us bow and pray: Dear Father in heaven, please forgive us for wanting those things which You have given to other people. Make us satisfied with what we have, and willing to help other people keep what is theirs. We ask this in Jesus' name. Amen.

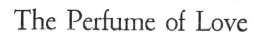

The Lord smelled a sweet perfume. Genesis 8:21

The Perfume of Love

Little Dan lived near a lake. One day he saw some flowers by the lake. "How pretty they look!" said Dan. "I'll pick some for my mommy and daddy."

Dan didn't know that these flowers were called skunk cabbage. They have a bad smell. Most people don't want them in the house.

When Dan brought the flowers to his mother, she said, "Thank you, Dan. You are very sweet." But his big sister said, "They have an awful smell! You aren't going to keep them in the house, are you, Mother?"

Her mother said, "They smell sweet to me because I smell the love of my little boy in them."

Did she really smell love? Can a person smell love?

15

Well, not really, but you know what Dan's mother meant. Even though the smell was bad, she liked the flowers because they told her that Dan loved her.

Noah burned an offering of thanks to God for saving him and his family from the Flood, and the Bible says, "The Lord smelled a sweet perfume." Does God smell offerings or fires? No, not as we do. But He knows the love that goes with the offerings. And He smells our love the way Dan's mother smelled his love.

In another place the Bible says, "Christ loved us and gave Himself up for us as an offering and a sacrifice to God, a sweet-smelling perfume." Those who want to follow Jesus are told to be like Him by walking in His footsteps of love.

When we follow Jesus and when we love other people for Jesus' sake, then, says the Bible, "we are to God a sweet perfume of Christ." Does that mean God can smell us? No, not as with a nose. But God sees that we love Him, and it is the "perfume" of our love that God smells.

And when we love God because of what Jesus has done for us, He forgives all that isn't good, just as Dan's mother did. She took a skunk cabbage and said it smelled sweet because her boy's love was in it.

Questions to talk about: What kind of flowers did Dan see one day? Why did he pick them? Why did his mother say, "They smell sweet to me"? Why did God say that Noah's offering smelled sweet to Him? What kind of sweet-smelling offering did Jesus give for us? When do our offerings smell sweet to God?

Bible reading for those old enough to read: Genesis 8:18-22.

Our prayer: Heavenly Father, we are glad that You love us for Jesus' sake. Even though what we do isn't very good, may His love and our love of Him make everything we do smell like a sweet perfume to You. Amen.

You must not steal. Exodus 20:15

Fair Trading

Herbie was bouncing his new basketball in the alley behind his house. He had just gotten it for his birthday. Jack came riding by on his bike. He was older than Herbie and usually paid no attention to him. But when he saw Herbie's new ball, he stopped.

"Hi, Herbie," said Jack. "Where'd you get the new basketball?"

"I got it for my birthday," Herbie answered. He was a little surprised that Jack was so friendly.

"That's pretty nice," said Jack. "I've got a new knife. Wanna take a look at it?" asked Jack, holding up a 49-cent knife.

Herbie took a look at it. "That's real gold on the sides," said Jack. "Wouldn't you like to have a knife like this? Maybe we can make a trade. I'll trade you for your basketball."

"Would you really?" asked Herbie.

"Sure," said Jack.

17

That evening Jack asked his father to put up a basket for him so he could practice shooting the basketball. "Where'd you get the ball?" Jack's father asked him. Jack was ashamed to tell, but he finally told his father what he had done.

"Do you think that was a fair trade?" Jack's father asked him.

"No," said Jack. "I guess I cheated Herbie."

"Well, what do you think you ought to do about it?" asked his father.

"Guess I'd better take the ball back to him," said Jack.

"That's a good idea, son," said his father. "And next time be sure you make a fair trade. Cheating is stealing, and you know what God says about stealing."

"I'm sorry," said Jack. "That was a dirty trick."

"Well, be glad that God is willing to forgive this too," said his father, "and don't do it again."

Let's talk about this: What is God's commandment about stealing? Why is cheating a sin like stealing? How did Jack cheat Herbie? When is God willing to forgive stealing? Why? Instead of cheating or stealing, what do you think Jesus wants His children to do with things that belong to other people?

Bible reading: Acts 9:36-40, the story of a woman who gave things to people instead of stealing from them.

Our prayer: Dear Father in heaven, for Jesus' sake forgive us if we have ever cheated someone or tried to take what was not ours. Make us willing to help others keep what belongs to them. In Jesus' name we ask this. Amen.

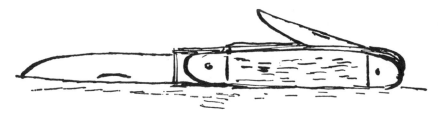

*The wisdom that is from above
is peaceable.* James 3:17

Why Mark Never Got Angry

"Hi there, Lanky-legs," yelled a boy from across the street. He wasn't trying to be mean. He just didn't know how cruel it can be to call other people names they don't like.

But it didn't seem to bother Mark. He just grinned and yelled back, "Lanky-legs will run you a race any time."

Mark never became angry when anyone called him names. "You can't ever pick a fight with Mark," his parents said.

"How come you're so easy to get along with?" one of his friends asked him one day.

"I learned a secret from my mother," said Mark. "One time when I was four years old somebody called me a dog. I cried and wanted my mother to hit him. But my mother said, 'People called Jesus many bad names, and Jesus never hurt them back. You want to be like Him, don't you?'

"Later that day she taught me a verse from her Bible. It said, 'The wisdom that is from above is peaceable.' 'If we are really wise, as wise as God can make us,' she told me, 'then nobody can make us angry or get us to quarrel and fight.'"

People treated Jesus much worse than anyone will ever treat us, and Jesus didn't fight them. He didn't even hate them. He forgave them. You see, Jesus came from heaven above to make peace between God and His people. Those who have His Spirit also try to get along peacefully with one another.

Questions to talk about: What did some boys call Mark? Why didn't he get angry? What secret did he learn from his mother? Which Bible verse did his mother teach him?

How did Jesus make peace between God and us? How can we become more peaceable, like Jesus?

Bible reading about wisdom: James 3:13-17.

Let us pray: Dear Jesus, we're glad that You are kind and peaceable. We're glad that You were willing to be hurt for us. Please make us wise and peaceable, too, so that we won't mind too much when people are mean to us. Help us to forgive others as You forgive us. Amen.

God shows His love for us in that, while we were
yet sinners, Christ died for us. Romans 5:8

How Good God Is

"You mean God hears everything I say, every word?" the new boy asked his teacher in Sunday school.

"Not only every word you *say*," said the teacher, "but every word you *think*."

"Like when I'm mad and think I'm going to run away — God hears what I think?" the boy asked.

"Yes, He does," said the teacher.

"Then I guess God doesn't like me," said the boy, " 'cause I think a lot of bad things."

"No," said the teacher, "that's what's so good about God. He knows how bad we are, but still He loves us. Do you want to learn a Bible verse about that?"

"Sure," said the boy. "I didn't know God was so good."

"Here's one from Romans 5:8. Why don't you sit down and copy it?" suggested the teacher.

While he was copying it, the other children looked up the verse in their Bibles and started learning it. It wasn't hard to learn. It said, *"God shows His love to us in that, while we were yet sinners, Christ died for us."*

The children said it; and the new boy said it too. Soon everybody knew it.

"I'm glad God loves people even though they are sinners," said the boy. "Otherwise He wouldn't love me."

Questions to talk about: What bothered the new boy in Sunday school? Why did the boy think God couldn't like him? What did the teacher tell the boy about God? Which Bible verse did the teacher find for the boy? What does it mean? Why did this verse make the boy happy?

Bible reading: Psalm 139:1-12.

Our prayer: Dear heavenly Father, we are glad that You love us even though we are sinners. We thank You for letting Jesus die for us to save us from our sins. Please forgive the many words we say which are not good. Help us to think good thoughts and say good words, for Jesus' sake. Amen.

Trust in the Lord. Psalm 37:3

Whistle, Don't Crawl

The weather was very cold, and the ice on the river was frozen clear down to the bottom. A man came walking down to the river. He wanted to cross where there was no bridge. "I wonder if this ice will hold me?" he said.

For a long time he looked at it and thought it would, but he wasn't sure. Then he said to himself, "If I crawl over, it won't break so easily." So he crawled over the ice on his stomach. The ice held him, but he was worried all the while.

On the other side the man saw a big truck coming down to the river. Without stopping, the truck drove on the ice and over the river. In the truck was a little boy riding along with his father. The boy never worried a bit that the ice would break. He was whistling a happy song all the while.

Which one was safer on the ice, the happy little boy or the scared little man? They were both safe. But there was a great difference between them. The boy who trusted his father was safe and happy. The man who did not trust the ice was safe but worried.

Some Christians are like the boy; others are like the man. Some trust that God will bring them across the way to heaven. They are happy with God and do not worry. Others are worried that they will lose their faith or that their faith isn't strong enough. So they crawl when they could ride and whistle.

You have Jesus, your Savior, with you every day. So trust Him. Be happy. Don't worry. Don't crawl. Ask Him to take care of you on your way to heaven. Then trust Him to get you there safely.

The Bible says, "You are kept by the power of God." So do what the psalm writer said, "Trust in the Lord." Then you'll feel like whistling.

Questions for conversation: How did the man cross the ice? Why? How did the boy cross the ice? Why did the boy whistle? What kind of Christians are like the man who crawled across the ice? Why can we be happy like the little boy? What does the Bible verse tell us?

A Bible reading about trusting the Lord: Psalm 91.

Our prayer: Thank You, dear Lord, for promising to take care of us on the way to heaven. Please help us to trust You more so that we will be happy with You on the way. Amen.

Without Jesus nothing was made that was made. John 1:3

When Mother Made Kool-Ade

Little Tommy was watching with big eyes. His mother took a pitcher of clear water, poured something into it from a small envelope, and suddenly the water was a very pretty purple. She had made Kool-ade. Tommy liked Kool-ade.

"Mother," said Tommy, "can you make wine out of water the way Jesus did?"

His mother smiled. "No, Tommy, I couldn't do that. Only Jesus could do that."

"But you made Kool-ade," said Tommy.

"I only added something to the water to make it taste good. Jesus changed the water into wine. That's much different," his mother explained.

"Jesus can do anything, can't He?" said Tommy.

"Yes, together with God the Father and the Holy Spirit, Jesus made all the water and the air and the land, all the stars, too, and the moon and the sun."

". . . and the trees and Kitty and me?" asked Tommy.

"Yes," his mother answered. "The Bible says, 'All things were made through Jesus, and without Him nothing was made that was made.' Most people don't know this. That's why they don't thank Him. Do you think you can remember the Bible verse?"

23

"Without Jesus nothing was made that was made," said Tommy, and his mother gave him a big glass of Kool-ade.

Some questions: What did Tommy's mother make out of water? How did she do it? What did Jesus once make out of water? How did He do it? What all has Jesus made, according to the Bible? So whom ought we to thank for the world and the things in it?

Bible reading: Hebrews 1:1-10.

Let us bow and pray: Lord Jesus, we thank You for all the things You have made for our good. We can see Your love for us in what You have made. We can see Your love especially in what You did for us when You died for us. We love You because You first loved us. Help us to live for You every day. Amen.

Whatever you do, do all to the glory of God. 1 Corinthians 10:31

How a Wrong Answer Was Right

A new pastor came to Grace Church one day. The first person he met was the cleaning lady.

"Good morning," he said, "I'm the new minister. And what work do you do for the Lord?"

She answered, "I do all my work for the Lord."

At first the minister thought that was a wrong answer. He expected her to say, "I clean the church" or "I teach Sunday school." But the more he thought about it, the more he liked what the cleaning lady had said.

That noon the pastor said to his wife, "I think the cleaning lady has the right idea. I'm going to preach a sermon about what she said."

So the very next Sunday he preached a sermon about the cleaning woman's answer to the question, "What are you doing for the Lord?" Can you guess what his Bible verse was? "Whatever you do, do all to the glory of God."

That's the way God wants us to live. Because we belong to Him, He wants us to do everything for Him. That's also the way we can be most happy. When we work for God, we don't really care how long a job takes or how hard it is or whether anyone says our work is good or not. We are happy to be doing something for God because we love Him.

Questions to talk about: What did the new pastor ask the cleaning lady? What did the lady answer? What did the pastor think about the answer? Which Bible verse did the minister use for his sermon the next Sunday? How can we do everything to the glory of God? What reasons do we have for doing everything for God?

Bible reading for grownups: Romans 12:6-13.

Our prayer: We are glad, dear heavenly Father, that we do not have to wait to do great things to honor You, but that we can serve You in whatever we do. Please help us to live all our life with You and for You out of love for Jesus, our Savior. Amen.

Bridle your tongue. James 1:26

A Bridle for Your Tongue

Roger and Irene were visiting their grandparents out on the farm. They went through the barn and saw some old harnesses.

"We used to put them on the horses so they could pull wagons and plows," said Grandpa.

"What's this little harness here?" asked Roger.

"That's the bridle," said Grandpa. "You see, this round piece of steel would go into the horse's mouth. It's called 'the bit.' And then this leather went over his head and ears to hold the bridle up. Lines would snap into the rings on both sides of the mouth."

"The lines were used to steer the horse, weren't they?" said Roger.

"Well, I guess you could call it steering," said Grandpa. "We called it driving. When you pulled the left line, the horse would go to the left. When you pulled the right line, he'd go to the right. By pulling both lines back, you could slow him up, keep him from running away, or make him stand still. That's how a bridle works."

"Now I see what Miss Adam meant," said Irene.

"What'd she say?" asked Grandpa.

"She said the Bible tells us to bridle our tongue," Irene explained.

"Thats a good idea," said Grandpa. "That little talking tongue needs a bridle to make it go the right way. And there's nothing more dangerous than a run-away tongue."

"How can I bridle my tongue?" asked Roger.

"Oh," said Grandpa. "That's easy. Just let Jesus put His 'bit' into your mouth, and let Him tell you what to say or not to say. That's the same as if Jesus were pulling the lines on a bridle for your tongue."

Questions to talk about: What's a bridle? Where did Roger and Irene see one? How are bridles used on horses? What does the Bible say we should bridle? Why do our tongues need to be bridled? What did Grandpa say is the best way to bridle the tongue?

Bible reading for older children and grownups: James 3:3-10.

Our prayer: Dear Father in heaven, we are sorry that our tongues often run away and say wrong words. Please forgive the many times we have sinned with our tongues. Bridle our tongues with the love of Jesus, and give us the Holy Spirit to help our tongues say what You want us to say. We ask this in the name of Jesus, our Lord and Savior. Amen.

The Word of God is alive and powerful. Hebrews 4:12

When God Talks to Our Hearts

Little Reba was on her mother's lap, listening to a Bible story. It was the story of Samuel. "Before he was born," said her mother, "Samuel's father and mother gave him to the Lord. They wanted him to belong to God."

Reba loved the story. When the story was over, Reba said, "Mother, you gave *me* to God before I was born, didn't you?"

Her mother blushed. "No, Honey," she said, "I'm afraid I didn't."

Reba felt like crying, but then she got an idea. "Can't you still do it, Mother? Can't you do it *now?*" she asked.

"Yes, dear," said her mother, "I can, and I have done it many times since you were born." Then she took Reba's hands in hers. "I want you to be God's girl," she said. "I want you to belong to Him all your life." Then little Reba was happy again.

You see, it wasn't only a Bible story Reba heard. She heard God talking to her through the story. She thought it was wonderful that Samuel was given to God. She wanted that wonderful thing to happen to her.

Our Bible verse says, "The Word of God is alive and powerful." Through His Word God talks to us and the Holy Spirit comes to us. When we listen to God talk to us through Bible stories and verses, something happens to us. God comes into our hearts and leads us to love Him. That's what happened to Reba.

God comes into our hearts especially when we hear about Jesus and His love. When we learn how Jesus died to save us from our sins, then we become sorry about our sins, and we want Him to save us and to change us. And He does.

The Word of God is alive and powerful. In another place the apostle Paul says, "It is the power by which God saves." That's why it's so important to hear and read and learn the Word of God every day.

Let's talk about this: What Bible story did Reba hear? What did Reba ask her mother? How did Reba's mother give her to God? What did Reba hear besides just a story? How does God talk to us? What happens when God talks to our hearts?

Bible reading: 1 Samuel 1:21-28.

Let us pray: Dear Father in heaven, we're glad that we are Your children. Whenever we hear Your Word, help us to hear more than just the words. Come into our hearts and change us for Jesus' sake. Amen.

Sing to the Lord. Psalm 96:2

Nickels for Rats

When Charles Spurgeon was a boy, he lived in a place where there were many rats. His mother hated rats. His mother also wanted her boy to learn hymns. So she paid him a nickel for every rat he killed, and a nickel for every hymn he learned. (It wasn't exactly a nickel, because it was English money, but that was about it.)

How would you like to get a nickel for every hymn you learn? Would you learn more of them if you got a nickel for each one? You ought to learn as many as you can without nickels, because they will do you more good than a pail of nickels.

Spurgeon later became a great preacher. He said he made more money killing rats than learning hymns, but the hymns did him much more good.

Next time you're in trouble, try singing a hymn. Next time you feel hurt, sing a hymn. Next time, instead of worrying, sing a hymn. Hymns help to keep God in your heart.

When you sing hymns, sing them to the Lord. The psalm verse says, "Sing to the Lord." Another psalm says, "Make a joyful noise to the Lord." Your singing doesn't have to be good. Maybe other people will call it noise. But God will be glad when you sing to Him.

We have lots of reasons for singing to the Lord. He saved us by dying for us. He loves us. He has made us God's children. "Sing to the Lord." Knowing hymns helps us do that.

Let's talk about this: For what did Spurgeon's mother give him nickels? What are some better reasons for learning hymns? What hymns can you sing without a book?

What does the psalm verse say? What are some reasons for singing to the Lord?

Bible reading: Psalm 96.

Our prayer: Lord God, we thank You for the people who have written good hymns for us to sing. You have given us many reasons for singing to You. Give us the Holy Spirit so that we will want to learn hymns and make a joyful noise by singing to You. Amen.

Come, Lord Jesus. Revelation 22:20

When He Comes

Little Susie was standing by the window with her nose pressed against the glass. It was after 5:00 o'clock. It was almost time for Susie's daddy to come home from work. Susie loved her daddy very much and often stood by the window in the evening so she could see him coming home.

"Mommy, what time is it? Isn't it time for Daddy to be here?" she asked. "I wish he'd come."

When Susie's dad did come up the walk, she ran out to meet him. He took her in his arms and carried her into the house. Now Susie was happy. Her daddy had come home.

Did you know that we are waiting for someone? Somebody special? He has been away a long time, but we are sure that He is coming back. We are waiting for Jesus. Before Jesus went up to heaven, He promised that He would come again.

When Jesus comes, He will take us all to heaven to be with Him. That is why we are so happy that He is coming. We can be just like little Susie who couldn't wait for her daddy to come home.

It will be wonderful when Jesus comes again. He will take us in His arms to our home in heaven. That is why the last prayer in the Bible says, "Even so, come, Lord Jesus."

Let's talk about this: Why did little Susie look for her daddy to come home? How did she feel when he came? For whom are all of God's children waiting? Why will we be happy when Jesus comes again? What prayer does our Bible verse teach us to say?

Bible reading for older children and grownups: Revelation 22:12-17.

Let us pray: Dear Lord, we are glad that You are coming again. Come, Lord Jesus, and take us to heaven. Amen.

If we confess our sins, God . . .
   will forgive our sins. 1 John 1:9

When Tommy Confessed

Tommy had just come back from the grocery store. "Put the change in my purse, please," said Tommy's mother.

"O. K., Mom," said Tommy. When he found his mother's purse in her bedroom, he began putting the change into it. Then he noticed quite a few coins already in the purse.

"Mom will never know if I keep a dime," Tommy thought. "Besides, I deserve some money for going to the store." So he kept a dime for himself.

When Tommy came into the kitchen, his mother said, "Thank you for going to the store for me. I know you're saving to get a new softball, so you may take a dime for helping me."

Now Tommy felt ashamed of what he had done. "Mom,"

31

he said, "I already took a dime. I know I shouldn't have. I know it was stealing. I'm sorry I did it. Please forgive me."

"I'm glad you know it was wrong to take the dime," said his mother. "I'm also glad you admitted what you did. Of course I'll forgive you. Every day I do things I shouldn't do. So I must ask God to forgive me just as you asked me to forgive you. And He always does."

"How do you know He does?" asked Tommy.

"Because He sent Jesus to pay for our sins. The Bible tells us that God always forgives us for Jesus' sake when we're sorry for what we have done. *'If we confess our sins, God . . . will forgive our sins,'* says the Bible."

"I'm glad you and God love me so much that you both forgive me," said Tommy. Then he gave his mother a big hug and went and put the dime back into her purse.

Let's talk about this: What sin did Tommy do when he put his mother's change away? Why was he sorry about what he had done? How did he confess his sin? Why was Tommy's mother willing to forgive him? What does the Bible say about God forgiving our sins? Why did Tommy put the dime back into his mother's purse?

Bible reading for older children and grownups: Psalm 51:1-12.

Our prayer: Lord God, our Father in heaven, how glad we are that You are always willing to forgive our sins for Jesus' sake! Teach us to confess our sins every day so that we may enjoy Your love every day. In Jesus' name we ask this. Amen.

He who loves . . . knows God. He who does not love
does not know God, because God is Love. 1 John 4:7, 8

Getting to Know God

Larry's parents stopped living together and put him into an orphans' home. There he thought no one cared about him, so he ran away twice. Each time he soon got into trouble stealing food. When the police took him back to the orphans' home, he hated everybody.

One day Mr. and Mrs. Lea came to the orphans' home. They invited Larry to live with them. They said if he would like them and they would like him, they would adopt him after a while.

So Larry went to stay with the Leas. But he said to himself, "They don't love me and I don't love them. I'll do what they tell me to do, but I'm not going to let them fool me."

Well, the Leas tried to love Larry. They did everything they could for him. And Larry did what he was told to do, but he never smiled. He never said "Thank you" or "I love you." He never felt as though he belonged to them. He felt like a stranger in their house.

One day Mr. Lea said to his wife, "I'm afraid we'll have to give him up. We just can't win his heart."

That day Larry fell and broke his leg, and Mrs. Lea took him to the hospital. She also stayed with him at the hospital. Then for weeks after he came home Mr. Lea carried Larry up and down steps and around the house.

One day as he was being carried, Larry hugged Mr. Lea real hard for being so good to him. Then he cried and said "Thank you" and told them he wanted to be their boy so he could stay with them always.

Larry didn't really know how much Mr. and Mrs. Lea loved him until he began to love them. And he didn't enjoy their love and feel at home with them until he believed that they loved him. But, oh, how different everything seemed when he wanted to belong to them.

Without love we cannot feel at home with God either. Just doing some things God wants us to do will not make us His children. It won't even help us to know God.

But when we see and believe that He loves us, then we love Him and try to please Him. The Bible says, "He who loves . . . knows God. He who does not love does not know God, for God is Love."

Questions to talk about: Why was Larry unhappy at the orphans' home? What did Mr. and Mrs. Lea offer to do for Larry? Why did they think they would have to give him up? What changed Larry and made him want to belong to the Lea family? What makes us feel close to God? How can we be sure that He loves us?

Let us pray: We don't only want to obey You, dear God, but we want to enjoy *belonging* to you. Please help us to understand how good You really are so that we will always love You and will want to be Your children forever, through Jesus Christ, our Lord. Amen.

Let no bad talk come out of your mouth,
  but only that which is good. Ephesians 4:29

Afraid of a Little Lettuce

There was a big family dinner at the Smith house. The table in the dining room was much too small. Two other tables were set up. The three tables stretched all the way from the dining room through the living room.

Aunt Emily was at one end of the row of tables. Johnny was at the other end. Johnny looked across at Aunt Emily and smiled. Then he looked at her salad. It was a half peach on some lettuce. A little piece of lettuce was on the peach. Johnny couldn't see what it really was.

"Aunt Emily," he said, "is that a worm on your peach?"

Johnny didn't mean to say anything bad. But what do you know? Aunt Emily couldn't eat her peach after that. She knew the little green thing was only a sliver of lettuce, but now she couldn't eat it. She kept thinking about the worm Johnny had said it might be.

That's how strong words are. Johnny didn't tie Aunt Emily up or hold back her arm. He just talked. But his words kept her from eating.

Talk is often more powerful than we think. It can do a lot to people. It can do good and it can do harm. That's why the Bible tells us to be careful with our talk. In Ephesians 4 God says, "Let no bad talk come out of your mouth, but only that which is good."

Good talk is that which helps other people. And the best talk is that which helps other people get the love of God. Do you know what kind of talk that is? It is talk about Jesus and what He did for us and wants us to do for Him.

Some questions: Why couldn't Aunt Emily eat her peach? What else can words do to people? What kind of talk is bad? What kind of talking does the Bible verse tell us to do? When is our talk good? What is the best kind of talk? Why?

Now read what Jesus said about talk: Matthew 12:33-37.

Let us pray: Dear God, please forgive all the words we say that may hurt someone. Help us to know how powerful words can be, and teach us to say only words that do good. Make us willing to talk a lot about our Lord Jesus. In His name we ask it. Amen.

*Let the redeemed of the Lord
say so.* Psalm 107:2

What Would YOU Do?

It was the last day of school. All the books had been put away, but there was still a little time left.

So the teacher passed out some paper. Then she said to the children, "Now we shall have one more lesson. On your paper write down what you would do if this were the last day of your life. Or what would you do tomorrow if you knew you would die the next day."

The children began to write. Ronald wrote, "I'd be real nice to my sister so I could go to heaven." Jimmy wrote, "I'd have all the fun I could have. I'd eat a lot of ice cream and play and go swimming." Larry wrote, "If I had only one more day to live, I'd tell people about Jesus. You see, Jesus is my Savior, and I'd want other people to be saved, too."

Which boy wrote the best answer? Larry, of course. Ronald thought he could get to heaven by doing a few good things. Jimmy thought only about himself. Larry thought of Jesus and wanted to help others get to heaven.

The Bible says, "Believe on the Lord Jesus Christ, and you will be saved" (Acts 16:31). "Whoever believes in Him will not die, but will have everlasting life" (John 3:16). To believe in Jesus means to trust that He is the Lord God and the Savior of all. That's why Larry's answer was best of all.

The psalm verse says, "Let the redeemed of the Lord say so." What are they to say? They are to thank and praise God and say that they are redeemed, or saved. They should tell others that Jesus has saved the whole world by dying on the cross for all sins. Then more people will believe in Jesus and will be saved.

Let's think about this: What did the teacher ask her children to write? What did Ronald write? What did Jimmy write? What did Larry write? Why did Larry want to help save people? From what are people saved by Jesus? What does the psalm verse say?

Bible reading for older children and grownups: Psalm 107:1-9.

Our prayer: Dear Father in heaven, we are glad that we are saved and belong to You. Help us to tell others so that they will believe in Jesus and be saved, too. In Jesus' name we pray this. Amen.

A good man cares for the life of his animal,
but the love of the wicked is cruel. Proverbs 12:10

Your Pets and You

"Mr. Frank is giving collie pups away, Dad," said Tim. "May we have one?"

Tim's dad looked him in the eye and said, "Do you remember when we had a rabbit? Who had to feed him?"

"Mother did," said Tim, "but it'll be different this time."

His dad answered, "Once there was a boy who had a dog, but he never washed him, never fed him, and hardly ever played with him. He said he loved the dog, but he was really cruel to the animal."

"I won't be like that, Dad," Tim promised.

"Very well, then," said his dad. "But first I want you to learn a Bible verse. Get the Bible, Tim."

When Tim got the Bible, his dad asked him to find Proverbs 12:10. Then he said, "As soon as you know that verse from memory and can tell me what it means, let me know. Then we'll talk some more about the dog."

Tim learned the verse fast and soon was ready to explain it, too.

"The first part says, 'A good man cares for the life of his animal.' This means that we should give our animals enough to eat and clean water to drink and a nice warm place to stay, and should treat them well," said Tim.

"All right," said his dad. "You forgot to mention training the animal, but how about the second part of the verse?"

"The second part means that it's wicked to forget your pet and not give him enough to eat and a good place to stay. That would be cruel even if you loved him and liked to play with him," said Tim.

"Very good," said his dad. "Now how about promising to take good care of your animal?"

"I promise," said Tim, and so he got his puppy. Whenever he forgot to take care of his pet, his dad made him say the Bible verse he had learned.

Let's talk about this: What did Tim want? Which Bible verse did he have to learn? What did it mean? What kind of pets do you think Jesus might have had? How do you think Jesus treated His pets? Why will Christians want to be good to their animals?

Bible reading: Proverbs 12:10-15.

Let us pray: Please forgive us, dear heavenly Father, if we have been cruel to our animals by forgetting to take care of them or in other ways. Please give us more of Your Spirit and make us more kind also to our pets. We want to please Jesus in this way, too. Amen.

Don't let a child grow up
without correcting him. Proverbs 23:13

Why Cindy Wanted to Be Spanked

Cindy had been naughty, and she knew it. Twice in one week her daddy spanked her. She was little, but not too little to know why she was spanked.

Cindy told her little friend Walter about the spankings.

"I never get spanked," said Walter.

"Sometimes you should get spanked," said Cindy.

"Why?" asked Walter.

" 'Cause then you'd be easier to play with, and you'd grow up to be a better man and . . . and . . . you might get to be a Christian, too," Cindy explained.

"Do spankings make you a Christian?" asked Walter.

"No, but my daddy says I'd get spoiled if he didn't spank me when I'm real bad."

"I'm glad my dad doesn't spank me," said Walter.

"I'm glad my daddy spanks me when I need it," said Cindy. "I want to be good 'cause I belong to Jesus."

"Can't you belong to Him when you're bad?" asked Walter.

"Sure," said Cindy. "But you gotta be sorry about the bad things you do, and spankings help you to be sorry."

The Bible tells parents: "Don't let a child grow up without correcting him. If you spank him, he will not die. But if you spank him, you may save his life from hell." When children are naughty, spankings and other kinds of correcting help to keep them from becoming spoiled and wicked.

Good parents do not spank often because they are kind and love their children. But *because* they love God and their children, they try to correct their children when they do wrong.

And God's children don't mind being spanked when they need it, because it helps them grow up to be better persons.

Questions to think about: Why was Cindy glad she got spanked? What did Walter think about spankings? Who do you think was the better-behaved child? When we love Jesus, how do we feel about our badness? What does the Bible tell parents about correcting their children? Why shouldn't God's children mind being spanked when they need it?

Bible reading: Proverbs 23:22-25.

We bow and pray: Heavenly Father, make us glad to be punished when we do wrong, so that we will turn away from our sins and will stay close to You, through Jesus Christ, who died to save us. Amen.

Don't be a hearer who forgets,
but a doer who acts. James 1:25

A Good Listener

Mother was very much surprised. "Why, Grace, you have the table all set!" she said.

"Isn't that what Pastor told me to do in his sermon Sunday?" asked Grace. She was trying to act as though she weren't trying to surprise her mother.

"I don't remember that he said anything about setting the table," her mother answered.

"Well, he said that children can please God by helping their parents," Grace told her. By now she couldn't help showing how happy her good deed had made her.

Maybe Grace didn't know it, but she was also being

a good Bible listener. Did you know that the Bible says we should all be good Bible listeners?

The apostle James said, "Don't be a hearer who forgets, but a doer who acts." It doesn't help much to listen to a sermon if we don't do what the sermon says. Nor does it help to read the Bible or have family devotions if we don't try to live what we learn.

Grace was a hearer who acted when she set the table for her mother. How good a Bible listener are you? That depends on whether you do what it says.

Questions to talk about: Why did Grace set the table for her mother? How did it make her feel? What kind of Bible listener could we say Grace was? What kind of hearer of God's Word are we to be? Can you say the Bible verse?

Bible reading: James 1:22-27.

Our prayer: Dear God, we often do not do what You have said in the Bible. Please forgive us for Jesus' sake. Help us to do whatever we learn from You, so that we will be happy hearers and learners of Your Word. For Jesus' sake we ask it. Amen.

What shall I do that I may
have eternal life? Matthew 19:16

The Trouble Money Can Lead To

Billy Gordon was riding with his father in a taxi in New York City. As they passed a big church, Billy's father leaned forward and talked to the cab driver. "Did you ever go to this church?"

"Naw," said the driver. "I don't have time to go to

church. I'm too busy trying to make money. If this preacher can tell me how to get more money, I'll go hear him."

Billy's father was surprised at what the man said. "Loving money leads to all kinds of evil," he told the man. "That's a warning God gives us in His Word."

"Yeah," said the driver. "But I love it. Money is all that matters. If you've got it, you can buy what you want, and people treat you well. But if you're poor, you're nothing."

Billy's father shook his head. He felt sorry for the man. "I'm sure you can't buy God," he said, "and you need Him." But the driver just gave a little huff.

Later Billy and his father talked about the man. "Billy," said his father, "there are many things much more important than money. Can you name a few?"

Billy didn't have to think very long. "You and my mother and being well and being happy and God and —"

"Good for you," said Billy's father. "I'm glad these things are important to you. Nothing is more important than life with God. That's why we ought to pay most attention to what He says. You know what He says about life with Him, don't you?"

"Sure, Dad," said Billy. "Whoever believes that Jesus is his Savior has everlasting life. That's life with God."

"Good," said his father. "Don't ever let the love of money lead you away from Jesus. That's the worst thing that could happen to you."

Questions to think about: What did the taxi driver love more than God? Why? What showed that he wasn't a Christian? Why does God warn us about loving money? How may the love of money lead people to sin? What is the worst trouble money can lead us into?

The story about a young man who lost his life with God because he loved money more than he loved Jesus: Matthew 19:16-22.

Let us pray: Dear God and Father in heaven, we confess that we, too, have sometimes loved money more than we loved You. Please forgive us for Jesus' sake, because He died for this sin also. Lead us by the Holy Spirit to love You more than anything else, and save us from the sin of loving money. We ask this in Jesus' name. Amen.

Be doers of the Word,
and not hearers only. James 1:22

God's Mirror

"James Nelson, you go right to the bathroom and look in the mirror. You're a sight!" said Mrs. Nelson to her boy. He had been playing in the park, where it was muddy.

Jim went and looked in the mirror. There were mud spots dried all over his face. His clothes were muddy, too, and his hair was very mussed.

Just then he heard a whistle outside. His friend Tom wanted to play with him. So Jim ran from the bathroom and out the back door and forgot all about what he had seen in the mirror.

Looking into the mirror didn't do Jim much good, did it? Many people look into God's mirror that way. Even when they see the dirt in their life, they forget to do something about it.

Do you know what God's mirror is? It is God's Word. When a teacher teaches a Bible story, or the pastor preaches a sermon, or we have a family devotion, or we read our Bible, the Word of God is like a mirror.

For example, when we hear Jesus say, "Love one another as I have loved you," we can see that we haven't been as loving and kind as Jesus wants us to be. Or when the Bible says, "Be glad in the Lord always," but we've been grumpy, then we hear God saying how we ought to be. That's like looking into a mirror. The Word of God shows us what's wrong with us.

But it doesn't do any good to look into a mirror and then not do something about what we see. When our face is dirty, it needs to be washed. When our hair is mussed, it needs to be combed. When we see that God wants us to be kind, we need to quit being mean to people. When God tells us to be happy, we ought to quit being grumpy. The Bible says, "Be doers of the Word, and not hearers only."

How can we straighten out what we see in a mirror? We can wash our face with water. We can comb our hair with a comb. But to wash and straighten out our lives, we need to believe in Jesus and His love and follow His ways.

Questions to talk about: What did James Nelson see when he looked into a mirror? Why didn't the look in the mirror help him? What is God's mirror? How can we look into this mirror? Who is the only One who can wash away our sins? How does He do it? What can we do to keep our lives from getting messed up?

Bible reading for older children and grownups: Matthew 7:21-27.

Our prayer: Dear Father in heaven, please lead us to look into Your mirror often, and to ask Jesus to wash away our sins. Help us also to walk in the ways that are right and good, for Jesus' sake, so that our lives will remain clean. Amen.

*Touch not the unclean
thing.* 2 Corinthians 6:17

Books Can Kill

In a faraway country called India, a soldier went to the library. The book he wanted was on a high shelf. When he reached for it, he felt something bite him. He jerked the book down and a small snake fell out. Its bite was very dangerous.

The soldier quickly put his heel on the snake's head and killed it. But his hand puffed up, and he almost died from the poison.

There's another kind of poison in many books. In many stores careless people sell books that put poison into your mind when you read them.

Don't read bad books. They can make your mind sick. They can kill your life with God. Don't look at bad TV shows. They can hurt you very much by spoiling your heart. As a man said, "Don't eat dirt with your eyes."

If you knew there was a snake in a book, you wouldn't touch it, would you? If you knew you could get poisoned by bad television programs, you wouldn't watch them, would you?

In the Bible St. Paul gives us an even better reason for not touching or watching or reading anything unclean. He says to all who love Jesus, "You are the house of the living God. God said, 'I will live in them and walk in them, and I will be their God, and they shall be My people. . . . Therefore touch not the unclean thing. . . . And I will be a Father to you, and you shall be My sons and daughters,' says the Lord Almighty."

If we are Christians, we are children of God, and God is living in us. Let's not spoil that with anything dirty in what we think or see or do.

Let's talk about this: What was in the soldier's book? What did the poison do to him? What kind of poison is in some books? What does the Bible verse say? What do you think this means? What reason does St. Paul give for not reading or watching anything unclean?

Bible reading for older children and adults: 2 Corinthians 6:16-18.

We pray: Dear Lord, our God, please help us to know what is good for us to read and hear and see. Make us willing to turn away from what is dirty because we are Your children through Jesus Christ, our Lord. Amen.

Jesus said, This I command you,
that you love one another. John 15:17

The Perfect Paste

Rita, the neighbor lady, came over and showed Mrs. Martin a little box she had just received in the mail. "They fooled me," she said. "A newspaper ad offered to send a box of perfect paste free. And look what I got."

Mrs. Martin opened the box. Inside was a little piece of paper. On the paper was only one word: LOVE.

"The ad promised it would mend almost anything," said Rita, who was a little angry.

"Well," said Mrs. Martin, "what they said is true in a way. Love will mend almost anything, even broken hearts." Then they both laughed and Rita felt better.

People spend a lot of money for a nice house, for a TV in the house, for soft rugs and pretty furniture. But if they don't put love into their house, it can never be a happy home. If they could buy love for as much as a car costs, what a bargain that would be!

Love is the best paste in the world, especially Christian love. It glues a family together. It makes people kind and brings them close together again whenever anything comes between them.

Jesus said to His disciples, "This I command you, that you love one another." God is Love, so He wants us to love. And love does wonders.

So from now on, before saying that mean word, let's remember that God wants us to say words of love. Before we make that sour face, let's remember that God would rather see a smile. Before we slam the door in anger, let's think of the love God wants us to show, and close it gently — with a forgiving heart.

Love is the world's best paste — and it costs *nothing!* We can get all we need from God through Jesus free of charge.

Questions to talk about: What did the paper say was a perfect paste? In what way is this true? What are some ways in which we can use love in our home? What does Jesus command in our Bible verse? How can we get all the love we need?

Bible reading for grownups: John 14:12-17.

Our prayer: Dear God, we are glad that the very best thing for our home costs no money at all. Please make us willing to bring it into our home, and give us the Holy Spirit so that we will love as Jesus wants us to love. We ask this in Jesus' name. Amen.

Jesus said, *If a man loves Me,*
he will keep My words. John 14:23

Real Love

"I love you, Mother," said Ruth. Then she gave her mother a kiss and ran out to play. She didn't bother to do the little bit of work her mother had asked her to do.

"I love you, Mother," said Mark and gave his mother a kiss. Then he went over to his friend's house and forgot all about straightening up his room and cutting the lawn.

"I love you, Mother," said Jane. Then she helped her mother with the dishes and laughed and talked as they made the beds together. When the baby cried, Jane played with him until her mother could come to feed him.

Which of the three do you think loved Mother the most? Yes, it was the one who helped the most. It's so easy to *say,* "I love you," but what we *do* shows how much we *really* love.

And so it is with loving Jesus. Did you know what He said about it? He said, "If a man loves Me, he will keep My words." Those who really love Jesus will gladly do what He has said they should do.

The first thing Jesus wants people to do is to believe that He is their Lord and Savior. Then they will love Him and keep His other words, too. But real love is in doing, not in saying without doing.

Questions to talk about: Which of the three children loved their mother the most? How could you tell? What did Jesus say a person does if he really loves Jesus? How can we keep His words? What is the first thing Jesus wants us to do? How can we best show that we really believe in Jesus?

Bible reading: John 14:21-24.

Let us pray: Dear Lord Jesus, Your love for us wasn't only in words. You worked and suffered and died for us. Please forgive us for not always loving You by what we do. Give us the Holy Spirit so that we will love You by doing Your words. Amen.

The angel said, *Jesus is not here; for He is risen, as He said.* Matthew 28:6

Napoleon and Jesus

Long before your grandfather lived, a little man called Napoleon became a famous ruler of the country of France. His army won wars against many other people, so Napoleon and his country ruled many other countries.

But God didn't let Napoleon stay powerful. After a while

his soldiers lost a war, and the great ruler was captured and put on an island. There he had to stay until he died.

Years later the French people brought Napoleon's dead body back to France. They wanted to remember their great leader. They put his body in six coffins, one in the other, and placed it in a beautiful, big church.

Every day many people visit this church to look at the coffins in which Napoleon is buried. But Napoleon is dead. He cannot help the French people. Even when he was alive, he became great only by using force.

Jesus, our Leader, is much greater than Napoleon. He didn't force people to love Him. He died to save them. He also showed that He is more than just a man. He became alive again after He died and showed that He is God.

When the women friends of Jesus came to the place where He had been buried, they found the grave empty. In place of Jesus' dead body there was an angel who said, "He is not here; for He is risen, as He said He would."

What a great leader we Christians have! He's not someone who just lived long ago; He's still living today! He's not a proud ruler who *killed* people to become great. He is kind and loving. He made Himself a poor man even though He's the King of heaven and earth. He died on a cross to save the whole world.

That's why the empty grave where Jesus was buried is a more wonderful place than the church where Napoleon is buried. That's why we talk about Napoleon, but we *worship* and *pray* to Jesus.

Questions to talk about: Who was Napoleon? What happened to him? Where is he buried now? Why do people visit the church where he is buried? Why can't he help the French people any longer? Why is Jesus a much greater Leader than Napoleon ever was? How do Christians honor Jesus?

Bible reading: The Easter story — Matthew 28:1-9.

Our prayer: Lord Jesus, our living Savior and King, how glad we are that You rose from the dead and are not buried in a grave. We thank You, dear Jesus, for saving us from the punishment of our sins. Help us to remember that You are still living and that we can depend on You for help in any trouble. Someday take us to where You are in heaven, that we may live forever with You. Amen.

Knowing puffs up, but loving builds up. 1 Corinthians 8:1

The Best Report

"I'm the best one in our class," said Sammy Grayson as he showed his report card to his mother. "Do you know who the worst one is?" he asked. "Clara Lory. She almost never has her lessons finished, and sometimes she sleeps in class."

"I'm glad you have a good report," said Sammy's mother. "But Clara has a good report, too."

"She does? Did you see it?" asked Sammy.

"No, I didn't see it," said his mother. "But I heard it from her mother."

"Mothers don't give reports," said Sammy. He was glad 'cause he wanted to be the best.

"Clara's mother gave her a very good report," said Mrs. Grayson. "She told me that Clara helps her a lot. When she was sick, Clara stayed up and rocked her little baby brother during the night. She also cleaned the house and tried to make the meals for her daddy and mother and baby brother."

"Is that why she was so sleepy in school?" asked Sammy.

"Perhaps," said his mother. "Anyway, Clara is kind and good to her little brother."

"I guess maybe Clara has a better report than I," said Sammy, getting the point.

There's a Bible verse that says, "Knowing puffs up, but loving builds up." Report cards may tell about what we know but not how we love. When we know things but do not love, we become proud and think we are big. But when we love, we become really strong, strong in our character.

How can we become more loving instead of proud? By letting Jesus and His love live in our hearts. He is God, and God is Love.

Questions to think about: Who had the best report from the teacher? Who gave Clara a good report? What was her report? Whose report do you think God liked the best? What does the Bible say about just knowing things? How does loving build up a person? How can we become more loving?

Bible reading for grownups: 1 Corinthians 13. Say "love" if your Bible says "charity," because years ago "charity" meant "love."

A prayer for a loving heart: Dear Father in heaven, please help us to learn our lessons well so that we will be able to do our work well for You. Best of all, give us the Holy Spirit so that we will become great in being loving and helpful. Please do this in us for Jesus' sake. Amen.

*Our children should teach
their children.* Psalm 78:6

Teaching Dolls to Pray

Little Sandy had five little dolls. One day she had them all lined up along the side of her bed, on their knees, with their faces against the bed.

"What are they doing?" Sandy's mother asked her.

"Mother, they're praying," said Sandy, surprised that her mother would ask.

"For what are they praying?" asked her mother.

"They're praying for Joyce to get better so I can play with her again," Sandy answered.

"Let's all pray," said her mother and took little Sandy on her lap. "You and I and the dollies, let's all pray for Joyce."

"Dear God," they said, "please make Joyce well soon if it is Your will, and make her happy also while she's sick. Amen."

"I'm glad you pray for others," said Sandy's mother. "I'm glad for something else, too."

"For what, Mommie?" asked Sandy.

"For wanting your dollies to pray. When you're big and God gives you children, I hope you will teach them all to pray."

"I will," said Sandy, "and I'll want them to know the Bible stories and all about Jesus and the Ten Commandments and everything."

Her mother was glad that Sandy was planning to be a good Christian mother. God wants His children to teach their children the wonderful works that He has done. Do you know why? The psalm writer says, "So that they will set their hope in God and not forget the works of God, but keep His commandments."

Questions to talk about: What were the dolls doing? Can dolls really pray? Why was Sandy's mother glad to pray with Sandy and her dolls? What else does God want His children to teach their children? Who can say the psalm verse?

Bible reading: Psalm 78:1-7.

Our prayer: Dear God, please fill our minds with Your thinking and planning, so that when we are older, we will do what You have told us to do. Remind all parents to teach their children what You have done for them, so that they will trust in Your love and will keep Your commandments. Help us to do this also, for Jesus' sake. Amen.

My times are in God's hand. Psalm 31:15

Living in God's Hand

"Aren't you afraid to go where those wild people live?" Becky asked Miss Rogers. Miss Rogers was a teacher who was planning to work for God in the wild country of New Guinea. The people there sometimes ate their enemies.

"No, I'm not afraid," said Miss Rogers. "Why should I be?"

"Somebody might kill you," said Becky. "Or you may get sick far away from a hospital. Or a snake might bite you. I wouldn't like to live in that country. It's too dangerous."

"My times are in God's hand," said Miss Rogers. "That's a Bible verse. It means that God decides what happens to His children. My life is in God's hand, because I have put my life in His hand."

"But God doesn't expect me to go to New Guinea, does He?" asked Becky.

"I don't know what God expects of you, Becky," Miss Rogers answered. "But I'm sure God wants *me* to go to New Guinea, so I'm glad to go for Him. Jesus did much more than that for me. I don't have to worry, because I'll be living in God's hand."

That evening Becky began to do some thinking about what God might want her to do for Him. She wanted to live in God's hand, too. Now she knew that this meant following God's ways and doing His work, whatever that might be.

Let's talk about this: Did you ever see a little bird sit in someone's hand? Why doesn't it feel safe and happy? In whose hand did Miss Rogers say her times were? Why wasn't she afraid to go to New Guinea? Why did she want to go? What did Becky begin to think about that evening?

Bible reading for grownups: Romans 10:9-15.

Let us pray: Dear Father in heaven, please help us to remember that our times are in Your hand. Give us the Holy Spirit so that we'll gladly live in Your hand. Help us to trust the love which You give through Jesus, so that we will gladly work for You and not be afraid. This we ask in Jesus' name. Amen.

They changed God's truth into a lie. Romans 1:25

Changing Truth into Lies

"My mother is sick," Peter told the neighbor lady. "I asked God to make her well."

"Peter," said the neighbor lady, "your mother isn't sick. Nobody is ever really sick. They just think they're sick. And nobody ever dies."

"Jesus died," said Peter.

"No, He didn't," said the neighbor lady. "Nobody dies. They just become somebody else and keep on living. Here's a book for your mother to read. It will tell her that she isn't sick."

Peter said, "I'll take it to my mother, but I know she's sick, and I know that Jesus died. He died to pay for my sins. And He became alive again."

Peter went home and told his mother what the neighbor lady said. "Peter," said his mother, "those people mean well, but they don't believe the Bible. They'd rather believe books that have changed God's truth into a lie."

"I knew she was wrong all the time," said Peter.

"I'm glad you did," said his mother. "We'd be very foolish to trade God's truth for a lie."

"That isn't a good trade, is it?" said Peter.

"No," said his mother, "not even as good as when you traded your telescope for some marbles."

Let's talk about this: What did the neighbor lady believe? What did Peter believe? Who was right? How do we know who is right? What did Peter's mother tell him?

Bible reading for older children and grownups: Romans 1:18-25.

Our prayer: Lord God, please keep us from ever changing Your truth into a lie. Help all who believe lies to learn the truth, especially the truth about Jesus and life with You. We ask this in Jesus' name. Amen.

Love never stops. 1 Corinthians 13:8

For God, Not for Thanks

"I don't think I'll do any more favors for George. He never even says 'Thank you,'" said Paul to his father one evening.

"What kind of favors?" asked his father.

"Oh, like holding his books when he wants to take off his coat," said Paul.

"Why did you do these favors for him in the first place?" asked his father.

"Oh, 'cause I wanted to be nice to him, and I ought to be kind," said Paul.

"Well, if you ought to, don't you think you ought to even if he never says 'Thank you'?" asked his dad.

58

"He never does anything for me," said Paul.

"But if it's what you ought to do, does it depend on a thank-you?" his father asked again.

"I guess not, but it sure would be easier," said Paul.

"I'm sure it would," said his father; "but why don't you do good for God and not for thanks? You could say to yourself, 'I'm holding George's books for Jesus. I'm helping George because I'm a Christian.' Then you won't get tired of doing favors."

It's easy to show love when somebody is nice. But real Christian love goes on even when no love comes back. The Bible says, "Love never stops." That's a short Bible verse worth remembering — only three words. Say them over a few times. They will help you understand God's kind of love.

Some questions to talk about: Why did Paul get tired of doing good to his friend? What did Paul's father tell him? What does our Bible verse tell us about real love? From whom can we get the kind of love that never stops?

Bible reading for older children and grownups: Romans 12:9-21.

Our prayer: Heavenly Father, help us remember how good You are even to people who never thank You, and how Jesus died also for them. Make us willing to do good for Jesus' sake, whether we are thanked for it or not. Amen.

*Whoever knows how to do good and doesn't do it,
for him it is sin.* James 4:17

The Sin of Doing Nothing

Jim Do-Nothing lived near a road that passed over a little river. One year so much rain came that the bridge washed away.

"You'd better put some boards over the river so people won't have to walk through the water," Jim's mother told him.

But Jim was too lazy. "Why should I drag a heavy board down there for a bunch of other people?" he asked.

So Jim did nothing.

When people came down the road, they had to walk through the water. One man spoiled a good pair of shoes. A lady ruined her skirt. A boy got very sick because his feet got wet when it was cold.

Whose fault was it? Jim's, because he could have laid those boards over the river until the bridge was fixed.

Did Jim think he had done anything wrong. Oh, no. "Me?" Jim probably would have said. "I didn't do nothing." But Jim's sin was doing nothing when he could have done something good.

When you can do something good and you don't do it, that is sin. The Bible says, "Whoever knows how to do good and does not do it, for him it is sin." When someone says, "I didn't do nothing," that may mean he didn't do what he should have done.

Of course, Jesus died to pay for this kind of sin, too. And for Jesus' sake God will forgive also the sin of not doing good. But that's all the more reason why we ought to do all the good we can. Jesus wants us to do as much good as we can.

Questions to talk about: What should Jim have done? Why didn't he do it? How did his laziness hurt other people? Why was all this Jim's fault? Can you think of some other times when it is wrong to do nothing? Why is God willing to forgive also the sin of not doing good? What makes us willing to do good?

A Bible reading about two men who did nothing: Luke 10:30-37.

Let us bow our heads and pray: Dear Father in heaven, please help us to love people so much that we will not try to find excuses, but will gladly do all the good we can, as our Lord Jesus did. Amen.

God says, *Call on Me in the day of trouble.* Psalm 50:15

Mrs. Bain in Trouble

Mrs. Bain, the neighbor lady, was having a lot of trouble. Her husband had died, and she was behind in her house payments. The TV man was coming to take her TV away, and her little girl was sick.

"I just don't know what to do," said Mrs. Bain.

"We'll help you in any way we can, but why don't you also pray to God about it?" said Tom's mother.

"I wish I could," said Mrs. Bain, "but I don't think I ought to. You see, I haven't prayed to God for so long."

"Then isn't it high time to pray now?" asked Tom's mother.

Mrs. Bain said, "I forgot about God when things were going well. It isn't fair to think of God only when things don't go right."

"That's true," said Tom's mother, "but God wants you to pray to Him anyway."

"Are you sure God wants me to pray to Him?" asked Mrs. Bain. You could tell she wanted to do it.

"God says so," Tom's mother told her. "In the Bible He says, 'Call on Me in the day of trouble.' You look it up yourself. It's Psalm 50:15. And that isn't all He said. He also said, 'I will deliver you.' That's a promise to help and save you."

"I'm sorry I didn't stay in touch with God," said Mrs. Bain.

Tom's mother smiled. "God sometimes lets troubles come to us so we won't forget Him," she said. "You see, He wants to save us from our worst trouble — our sins and their punishment. That's why Jesus even died for us."

"Did Jesus really die for me, too?" asked Mrs. Bain.

"Yes, He did. The Bible says, 'He died for all.' And when you belong to Jesus, God forgives you your sins and loves you for Jesus' sake," Tom's mother told her.

"Then I will pray to God again. If He loves me, I'm sure He'll help me," said Mrs. Bain. That night Mrs. Bain called to God for help in her troubles.

Some questions: What kind of troubles did Mrs. Bain have? What did Tom's mother tell her to do? Why didn't she want to pray? With which words does God invite us to pray when we're in trouble? What does God promise to do for those who call to Him for help? How do you think He may have helped Mrs. Bain?

Bible reading for grownups: Psalm 130.

Our prayer: Dear God, thank You for letting us come to You in our prayers in Jesus' name. We are glad that You always answer us in some way, even though we don't deserve it. We thank You especially for promising to save us from our sins when we trust in Jesus. Amen.

*Who has known the mind
of the Lord?* Romans 11:34

How Jim Fixed a Clock

The kitchen clock was running a little slow.

"I'm going to save Mother some money; I'll fix it my-self," said Jim. So he took it apart and looked it over. But he couldn't see anything wrong or broken.

Then Jim tried to put the clock together again. When he was finished, he had three wheels left over, and he didn't know where they belonged. He also had two screws left. Now the clock wouldn't run at all.

"I guess I don't understand clocks," said Jim. "Can you get it fixed, Dad?" he asked. They took it to a man who knew how to fix clocks.

"You're a little like the people who think they under-stand God," Jim's father said to him on the way home from the clock man. "It isn't easy to understand even a clock, is it?"

Jim felt a little ashamed of what he had done. "I thought I knew how to fix it," he said.

"Yes, many people think they know all about everything," said his father. "They also think they know how God should do things. They even try to tell Him what to do."

"And they couldn't even figure out a clock if they had to," said Jim, laughing at himself.

"So let's trust God. He knows what He's doing, even when we can't understand Him," Jim's father told him. "The Bible says, 'Who has known the mind of the Lord?' "

"Jesus knows," said Jim, "because He is the Lord."

"Right you are," said his father. "That's why we'd better let Jesus tell us about God and life with Him."

Some questions to talk about: What did Jim try to fix? How come he had some wheels left over? What question does the Bible verse ask? What is the answer to that question? Where does God tell us what He wants us to know? How can we let the Lord decide things for us?

Bible reading for older children and grownups: Romans 11:33-36.

Let us bow before God in prayer: Dear heavenly Father, if we can't understand such little things as a clock, how can we hope to understand You? Please help us to trust You, no matter what happens, and to let You fix up our lives. We are glad that You love us for Jesus' sake, and that's really all we need to know. Amen.

*If we have food and clothes,
let us be satisfied.* 1 Timothy 6:8

When Nobody Was Satisfied

A rich man put a notice in a newspaper. It said: "I will give a house to the first person who is satisfied with what he has."

Many people came and asked for the house. When the man asked them why they wanted it, they told him that the house they had was too small, or that it wasn't their own, or that it wasn't paid for. They all wanted something better than they had.

"You're not satisfied with what you have," the man told these people. So he gave the house to a poor widow with five children who was working hard and didn't come and ask for the house.

Are most people satisfied? No, they aren't. When they have a car, they soon want a better one. When they have a job, they wish they didn't have to work. When they don't have something to do, they wish they could work.

Children, too, are often not satisfied. When they're on a trip, they want to be at home. When they're at home, they want to go somewhere. Little children get unhappy very easily when they can't have what they see.

It isn't always wrong to want things. Jesus even told us to ask Him for much more than we do. But God does not want us to be unhappy if we cannot have what we want.

As long as we have enough to eat and enough to wear and a place to be at home in, we ought to be satisfied. If God gives us more, we can be thankful. If that's all He wants us to have, it's best not to have more. That's why the apostle Paul says in our Bible verse: "If we have food and clothes, let us be satisfied."

Let's talk about this: What did a rich man say in a newspaper? Why didn't the people who came get the house? Who got it? Why are most people never satisfied? Why can we be satisfied with whatever God gives us? What did the apostle Paul tell Timothy in the Bible verse?

Bible reading: 1 Timothy 6:6-11.

Let us pray: Dear Lord God, we thank You for the many things You have given us. Please forgive our grumbling and complaining. Help us to be thankful and busy for You, but make us satisfied with whatever You give us. We ask this in Jesus' name. Amen.

The apostle Paul said, *We make many people rich.* 2 Corinthians 6:10

How to Make Others Rich

"I'm going to marry Dan Harris; he'll make me rich," said Mary Jane's sister. Not long after this she married him. And because Dan Harris was rich, he made her rich.

But the two weren't happy together. They didn't love each other. Making someone rich with money doesn't always make him happy.

In the Bible the apostle Paul tells of another way of making people rich. Even a poor person can make someone else rich the Bible way. Though St. Paul was poor, he wrote, "We make many people rich."

What did Paul mean? How did he make many people rich? He and his helpers were poor people. They didn't have much money. They didn't own a lot of buildings or a big business.

Paul told people about Jesus. He led them to trust in Jesus as their Savior. From Jesus they received the forgiveness of their sins and a place in heaven. That's worth lots more than a million dollars.

Jesus also gives people peace with God and joy in their hearts. He fills their hearts with love and makes them good. This makes their hearts rich.

We can make people rich, just as Paul did, by helping them to find Jesus and His love. We, too, can make people rich even when we are poor.

Questions to think about: Why did the girl marry Dan? How did he make her rich? Why didn't that make her happy? Who said he was poor but made many people rich? How did the apostle Paul make many people rich? How can we make people rich as he did?

Grownups may now want to read: 2 Corinthians 6:1-10.

Our prayer: Dear Jesus, thank You for giving us forgiveness of sins and a happy and good life with God. Help us to make other people rich in the same way by giving Your love to them. Amen.

God loves a cheerful
giver. 2 Corinthians 9:7

The Happy Giver

"If you had a million dollars, would you give them to Jesus?" the Sunday school teacher asked her pupils.

They all said they would.

"If you had $500, would you give $300 to Jesus?"

"Yes," they all said, "we would."

"If you had one dollar, would you give part of it to Jesus?"

The boys and girls looked at each other. "Yes," said Timmy. (You see, Timmy had no dollar.) "I would," said Jerry, and he took a quarter out of his pocket and offered to give it. The others kept quiet. They had a dollar at home, but they didn't want to give part of it away, not even for missions.

The children all said they would give a million because they didn't have it. But most of them didn't want to give what they could.

It's easy to say what we would do for Jesus if we had a million. But how much will we do for Jesus with what we have? That is the real question and the real test. Our love of God is shown by what we are willing to do for Him right here and now. And our giving doesn't have to be just money.

Love makes us want to *do* things for Jesus. And Jesus wants us to give money or anything else to Him because we love Him, not because we think we have to. The Bible says, "God loves a cheerful giver." Cheerful givers are people who give because they want to. Their love makes them happy givers.

Let's talk about this: Why was the class willing to give a million? Why didn't most of the children want to give part of one dollar? What do you think Jesus cares about most of all — our money or our love? Why are people who love Jesus cheerful givers? Let's say the Bible verse together.

The story of a woman who loved Jesus: Luke 7:36-50.

Our prayer: Dear Jesus, help us remember that You love a cheerful giver. Make us glad to do what we can for You and for other people because we love You. Amen.

The Lord said to Elijah, "Go show yourself to Ahab."
And Elijah went. 1 Kings 18:1, 2

A Very Brave Person

Jack was a little boy. The first time his parents wanted him to go to Sunday school by himself he didn't want to go. He was afraid. He cried. But his mother said, "Jesus wants you to go." So Jack went.

Jack was brave that morning he went to Sunday school alone for the first time. A person has to be brave to go where he is afraid to go. When Jack gets big, maybe he will be as brave as the prophet Elijah was long ago.

Elijah told King Ahab and his wicked queen that there would be no rain for a long time. God was punishing them and their country for not obeying Him. Then for three years it didn't rain, and the king and the queen blamed Elijah for this. They wanted to kill him and looked everywhere for him, but nobody knew where he was. He was safe. God had told him where to hide.

One day the Lord said to Elijah, "Go show yourself to Ahab." But that would be very dangerous. He might get killed. Ahab had already killed most of the other prophets of the Lord. But the Bible says, "Elijah went." He didn't give any excuses. Because God told him to go, he went.

Those two words, "Elijah went," tell us what a brave man Elijah was. Elijah trusted God very much when he went to the king who wanted to kill him.

There are times when we also will have to be brave for God. To be brave doesn't mean doing things without being afraid. Brave people are sometimes very much afraid. But when we are afraid and do what God wants anyhow, that is being brave.

Sometimes it takes a very brave person just to say "No" when other people want him to say "Yes" to something wrong. Sometimes a person has to be very brave to do what God wants him to do.

Some boys wanted Tom to steal a bicycle. When Tom refused, they said, "You're chicken!" But Tom was brave. He didn't steal just because someone called him "chicken."

God helps His children to be brave when they love Him and trust in Him. And He takes care of them, too, just as He took care of Elijah.

Let's talk about this: What was the brave prophet's name? Why was he hiding? What did God say to him? What does the Bible say Elijah did? Can you think of something brave we could do for God?

Bible reading for older children and grownups: 1 Kings 17:1-6; 18:1-8, 17, 18.

Let us pray: Dear Father in heaven, so often we are cowards when we should be brave. Please forgive us for Jesus' sake. Make us brave enough to do whatever You want us to do. We ask this in Jesus' name, who was brave enough even to die for us. Amen.

If One died for all, then all have died. 2 Corinthians 5:14

All Paid Up

The whole gang of boys and girls was in trouble. They had gone fishing where they weren't allowed to fish. They had thought it was all right, but it wasn't. It was against the law, and they were caught. So now each one of them had to pay a $10 fine.

Mary and Jack and some of the others didn't have $10. "I don't even have five dollars," said Jack. The gang was talking about the problem at Mary's house.

Mary's father felt sorry for them. So he said, "I'll pay your fines for you."

"All of ours?" asked Jack. "Mine, too?"

"Yes, yours, too," he said.

"Oh, thanks a lot," said Jack. "Thanks a lot." All the others also said "Thank you" to Mary's father. "Boy, do you have a good father!" they said to Mary.

The next day when the newspaper came, Jack said, "Say, here's my name and all of our names. It says we all paid our fines. But we never really did. Mary's father paid them all."

"Well, Jack," said his mother, "if he paid the fine for you, that's the same as if you paid it. And if he paid for all, then all of you have paid."

"Isn't that swell!" said Jack.

"This reminds me of what Jesus did for all of us," said his mother. "He paid the fines we owe God for breaking His laws. He didn't just pay money; He gave His life."

Jesus died for us to pay our fines. The Bible says, "He died for all." It also says, "If One died for all, then all have died." Because Jesus died for all, our fines are all paid. It's just as if we ourselves had died to pay for our sins.

Let's talk about this: What had Jack's gang done wrong? What was the punishment? Who paid it? What did they think of Mary's father? What did the newspaper say? Who died to pay for what we have done wrong? What does our Bible verse say? How does this make us feel toward Jesus?

Bible reading for grownups: 2 Corinthians 5:14-21.

Our prayer of thanks: Dear Jesus, how can we ever thank You enough for dying for us? Because You died for all of us, we have died and paid for our sins. Help us to understand this and to show our thanks to You by not sinning. Amen.

Even Christ pleased not Himself. Romans 15:3

Me First?

Bob was the leader, and he wanted things his way.

"Now we'll play hide-and-go-seek," he said, and they all did.

"Now we'll play ranch, and I'll be the rancher," he said. So they played ranch.

By and by Bob's friends got tired of playing only his way. "Let's play something else," they said.

But Bob wouldn't listen. "You have to do what I want," he said. "I'm the leader."

So one after another the friends went to Bill's house and played there.

When Bob was left all alone, he went inside and told his mother about it.

72

"No wonder they left you," she said. "Nobody likes people who always want their own way."

"Would Jesus let other people have their way?" asked Bob.

"He certainly would in a game," said Bob's mother. "The Bible says, 'Even Christ pleased not Himself.' Whatever He did, He did to please His Father or us. He even suffered and died for us."

Then Bob decided he would try to please the other boys and girls, not just himself. He would do it first of all to please Jesus. When he tried it, he found out that it made others happy to be with him. This made him happier, too.

Some questions to talk about: How did Bob try to please himself? Why did his friends go to Bill's house? What did Bob's mother tell him? What did Bob decide to do? What happened when he stopped trying to please himself? How did Jesus please His Father for us?

Bible reading for older children and grownups: Philippians 2:1-11.

Our prayer: Lord Jesus, we're glad You didn't live to please Yourself, but even died for us. Please give us a love like Yours so that we will want to please You in everything we do. Make us want to please other people, too, and not just ourselves; for Your sake. Amen.

Lay up for yourselves treasures in heaven. Matthew 6:20

Treasures in Heaven

Once there were two brothers who grew up together in the country called England. One of them became a businessman and made lots of money. But when he died, very few people cared, and hardly anyone ever thinks about him any more.

The other brother became a missionary doctor and went to Africa. He never had much money. He died a poor man. But he was rich in another way. People still talk about him a lot.

The man in Africa was David Livingstone. He helped many people. He taught them about Jesus. He explored the country of Africa. He helped many slaves get free. Because of what he did for God and people, he is buried in a church in England along with kings and other great men.

If it hadn't been for David, we probably never would have heard about his brother. When the brother died, people said, "He was David Livingstone's brother."

Of course, David Livingstone's brother may have had some of God's treasures, too, but which brother do you think had the best life? What kind of treasures would you rather have a lot of at the end of your life?

Jesus said, "Lay not up for yourselves treasures on earth." Don't spend your time just trying to get money or other things that thieves can steal. "But lay up for yourselves treasures in heaven." Get lots of God's love and God's Spirit. Thieves cannot steal God's love. We can all have treasures in heaven by living with Jesus and by serving Him.

74

Let's talk about this: How did one of the brothers get rich? Why did the other brother remain poor? Where was the missionary's treasure? Which of the two brothers did the most for other people? What did Jesus say about treasures? What did He mean?

Older children and grownups may now read: Matthew 6:19-34.

Our prayer: Dear Father in heaven, please lead us to lay up treasures in heaven. More than anything we want Your love and Spirit. It is worth more than all the money in the world. By Your love please make us rich in good works, for Jesus' sake. Amen.

The person who gets angry easily acts foolishly. Proverbs 14:17

Keep Your Temper: No One Wants It

"You get out of here," said Peter to his sister and pushed her hard. She fell against the sewing machine and hit her head. It started to bleed.

Peter got scared and ran outside. His sister went screaming to her mother. She washed the cut and put a band-aid on it.

Peter's mother said nothing to him until later that afternoon. When his sister was sleeping, Peter came quietly back into the house and asked about her. He was worried and sorry.

His mother put her arm around him and said, "Son, don't you wish you didn't have that quick temper?"

"Yes," he said.

75

"Someday you might hurt somebody real bad by getting angry so easily."

"I said I was sorry," Peter whined. But he meant it.

"Then let's ask God to keep us from getting angry," said Peter's mother. And so they prayed that God would forgive Peter for Jesus' sake. They also asked God to help Peter control his temper.

The Bible says, "The person who gets angry easily acts foolishly." When we get angry easily and lose our temper, we do wrong things that we wouldn't do otherwise.

Jesus came to help us keep our temper and to save us from hurting ourselves and others. He had to die to pay for the foolish things we do when we lose our temper. Those who keep Jesus in their heart learn to keep their temper.

Questions to talk about: Why did Peter push his sister? What happened to her? Why was Peter sorry? How did his mother try to help him? Would a spanking have helped him more? What makes you think so? What does the Bible verse say about a person who gets angry easily? What can keep us from getting angry easily?

A Bible reading about what an angry person once did: Genesis 4:1-8.

Let us pray: Dear Father in heaven, we know that You do not want people to have a bad temper. Please help us to control ours so that we will not do anything foolish by getting angry easily. Forgive our sins and make us easy to live with, for Jesus' sake. Amen.

The will of the Lord be done. Acts 21:14

When Sally Grumbled

Sally was standing by a window in her house, grumbling.

"I don't see why we can't have our picnic," she said. "I prayed for a nice day, and look at it rain!"

"Maybe somebody else prayed for rain," said her brother, teasing her.

Sally pushed her lip out farther. Then she turned to her mother. "Mother, why didn't Jesus let us have a good day? I prayed for it."

"He did give us a good day," said her mother. "A rainy day is a good day. Today the strawberries are growing, so you can have strawberry jam. Today the grass is growing out in the country, so you can have milk and meat from cows, who need grass. Today the streets are being washed clean of dust and dirt. Oh, it's a good day," said her mother.

"But I want to have a picnic," Sally pouted.

"It isn't always good to get what we want, Honey," said her mother. "You prayed for a good day for your picnic, but maybe Mr. Miller prayed for rain for his garden. What do you think God should do if gardens need rain and you want a picnic?"

"Well, all right," said Sally without answering the question. "Let's have a picnic *tomorrow*."

"Good girl," said her mother.

When some Christians in the Bible noticed that they couldn't have their way, they said, "Let the will of the Lord be done." We know that God loves us for Jesus' sake, so we can say to Him, "Thy will be done." When we say this and mean it, we can be happy, no matter what happens. Let the will of the Lord be done.

Some questions: Why was Sally grumbling? How could Sally's mother say it was a good day? Why isn't it always good to get what we want? Whose will is always good? What did some Christians in the Bible say should be done? Why ought we be willing to say to God, "Thy will be done"? How will this help us?

Bible reading: 2 Corinthians 12:7-10.

Let us bow in prayer: Please forgive us, dear God, for sometimes having grumbled over what You decide. We are glad that You know what is best. Please help us to be willing to take things Your way and to say, "Thy will be done." We ask this in Jesus' name. Amen.

Whoever keeps the whole Law, but fails in one point, has become guilty of all *of it.* James 2:10

The Lawbreaker

Mr. Gordon was trying to show his girl Sally that all people are sinners, and that she did wrong things, too. "Once in a while I do something wrong," Sally admitted, "but I do a lot of good things, too."

"Well, now," said her father, "suppose my secretary passed my desk fifty times, and each time she wanted to take ten dollars out of it, but she didn't. Would you call that being good fifty times?"

"Yes," said Sally.

"But suppose the next time, when I wasn't there, she opened the desk and stole ten dollars," said Mr. Gordon. "Would she be a thief or not?"

"She'd be a thief," said Sally. She was beginning to catch on.

"But she didn't steal fifty times, and she stole only one time. Why don't you say she is fifty times better than a thief?" he asked.

"Well," said Sally, "she's a thief even if she stole only once."

"Right," said Mr. Gordon, "and that's the way God figures, too. He says, 'Whoever keeps the whole Law, but fails in one point, he is guilty of breaking *all* of it."

"Then I'm guilty of breaking God's Law, too," said Sally.

"Yes," said her father. "That's what the Bible means when it says, 'All have sinned.' We are all sinners, and we all need God's forgiveness. And God is always willing to forgive us for Jesus' sake. But we have to admit that we have done wrong so that we'll want His forgiveness."

"I admit it," said Sally, "and I'm glad that Jesus forgives."

Questions for conversation: Why did Sally think she was good? What would have made the secretary a thief? What does the Bible verse say about anyone who breaks a single law of God? Why do we all need God's forgiveness? Why is God willing to forgive us? How did this make Sally feel?

Bible reading: James 2:8-13.

Our prayer: Holy Spirit, please help us to know that we are sinners so that we will know how much we need our Savior Jesus. May we show our thanks for His forgiveness in all that we do. Amen.

Remembering that We Are Dust

"Daddy," said Billy when he came home from school one day, "why does the Bible say, 'God remembers that we are dusty'?"

"Oh, it doesn't say that," said his dad. "You must have gotten something wrong."

"It does too say that," said Billy, and he ran and got his Bible. Quickly he looked for Psalm 103. His teacher had read that psalm in school that day.

Billy's dad looked at the psalm. "Read verse 14 again, Billy," he said. "Does it say we are dusty?"

Billy couldn't read real well yet; he was only in second grade. But he could make it out: "God remembers that we are dusty, no, dust."

"That's different, isn't it?" said his father. "When God made the first man, how did God make him?"

"He took some ground and maybe mixed it with water, and shaped it like a man. Then God breathed into him to make him alive," Billy explained.

"Good boy, you remember the story," said his father. "So Adam was made out of ground. Dry ground is called dust. Adam's body wasn't made out of some heavenly stuff. And neither are we. So when we do something wrong, God remembers that we are dust. That means, God knows how weak we are and how easy it is for us to sin."

This is why the Bible says in the same verse, "Like a father feels sorry for children, so the Lord feels sorry for those who fear Him." He sent His Son Jesus to save us, and for Jesus' sake He forgives our sins and helps us. How glad we can be that God remembers we are made out of dust.

80

Questions to answer: What mistake did Billy make in reading the Bible verse? How did God make the first man? What does God mean by saying He remembers that we are dust? What has He done for us because He feels sorry for us? Why is He willing to keep on forgiving us?

Bible reading: Psalm 103:8-14.

Let us pray: Lord, our God, You know how easy it is for us to sin. Have mercy on us, Lord. For the sake of Jesus please forgive all our sins, as You have promised. Help us to act like Your children in all that we do, even though we are weak and sinful. In Jesus' name we ask it. Amen.

The unmarried woman will have more children than the married wife. Isaiah 54:1

A Family of 48 Children

Rose was just 22 years old when she finished college and decided to go to a faraway heathen island to be a Christian teacher.

"Don't do it," her friends told her. "You won't have much chance to get married if you go way out there."

"But I think God wants me to go there," said Rose, and she went anyway.

Rose never did marry. But because she loved God and children, God gave her more children than most married women ever have. This is how it happened:

One day God gave a heathen mother twins. The people thought a bad spirit had made one of them. So they laid the twins under some bushes in the woods and left them both to die. Rose found them and took them home.

On another day a mother chased her boy out of his home and told him never to come back. So Rose gave him a place in her home and took care of him.

That's the way Rose's family started to grow. By and by Rose needed a big house for all her "children." Before she died, she had 48 of them. From her they all learned to love Jesus, and many of them now are missionaries on that island.

Long ago God's prophet said, "The unmarried woman will have more children than the married wife." God often gives big families also to unmarried people who love and help others.

And there is another way in which God gives children to His people. When girls or boys learn to love Jesus, they are born again. They become Christians. And if we have helped them to become God's children, then in a way they are also our children.

Questions to talk about: Where did Rose go? What did she do for some twin babies? How did her family grow? How can an unmarried woman have more children than a married wife? What can we do to help people become God's children?

Bible reading for older children and grownups: Isaiah 54:1-5.

Let us bow and pray: Dear Father above, we are glad that You have made us a part of Your big family. Give us the Holy Spirit so that we will gladly help other people, especially children, who need our love. We ask this in Jesus' name. Amen.

Seek the Lord while He may be found.
Call on Him while He is near. Isaiah 55:6

Let's Not Be Too Late

"Mr. Groot is next door, visiting his relatives," said Jerry. "I hope he'll let me come to his farm this summer. I love to ride horses and hunt eggs and watch the pigs."

"Well, then you'd better go talk to him," said Jerry's mother.

"I will," said Jerry, "as soon as I've read this story."

When he finished the story, Jerry started putting an airplane together. "Better see Mr. Groot now," said his mother.

"I will, as soon as I've finished my model airplane," said Jerry. When Jerry finally went to see Mr. Groot, Mr. Groot was gone. So Jerry didn't get to go to his farm.

Some people think they have plenty of time to get to know God. Even though they want to live with Him in heaven, they always have something else to do that seems more important than calling on God here on earth. Some of them die without ever meeting God or getting acquainted with Him. So they miss going to heaven.

That's why the great prophet Isaiah says: "Seek the Lord while He may be found. Call on Him while He is near."

In the next verse he also tells us how to call on God: By leaving our sins and asking God to forgive us and to love us. When we do that, the prophet says, "The Lord will have mercy." For Jesus' sake He will come and live in us and will give us a happy life both here on earth and in heaven.

Questions to talk about: How did Jerry lose his chance to have fun on Mr. Groot's farm? Why do some people put off getting to know God real well? When are we to call on God, according to the prophet Isaiah? What may happen to people who do not seek the Lord?

Bible reading: Isaiah 55:1-7.

Let us pray: Heavenly Father, have mercy and forgive us for visiting with You so little, even though You are always near and want to love us through Your Son Jesus, our Savior. Please turn us away from all sins, and give us a happy life with You both now and forever in heaven. In Jesus' name we ask it. Amen.

When I am afraid,
  I will trust in God. Psalm 56:3

In the Operating Room

A little boy was very sick. He was on the operating table in the hospital. The doctor had to take out his appendix so he could get well. A nurse was ready to give him some funny-smelling gas so the operation wouldn't hurt.

"Are you going to put me to sleep?" asked the boy.

"Yes," said the doctor.

"Well, I always pray before I go to sleep," said the boy. "May I pray first?"

"Yes," said the doctor.

So the boy prayed: "Dear Jesus, please be with me also while I am asleep. Help the doctor do his work right. I know that You love me, dear Jesus, so please take care of me. Amen."

Then the boy smiled, and the nurse put him to sleep.

Jesus blessed the operation, and soon the boy was well. When he was ready to go home from the hospital, the doctor said to his father, "I wish more grown-up people would be as close to God as your boy. I don't think you were afraid, were you, son?"

"No," said the boy, "I wasn't afraid, because I asked Jesus to be with me, and I knew He would be. Nothing could go wrong. If I had died, I would have gone to heaven."

The psalm writer said, "When I am afraid, I will trust in God." In another psalm King David said to God, "Those who know You will put their trust in You."

Because the little boy knew that God loved him, he

85

trusted that God would let nothing bad happen to him. That's why he wasn't afraid even of his operation.

Some questions: Why was the little boy in the hospital? What did he ask the doctor before he was put to sleep? What did he say to Jesus? Why wasn't he afraid? Why wasn't he afraid even though he could have died? Who can say the Bible verse?

Bible reading for those who can read well: Philippians 1:19-21.

Let us pray: Dear God, we are glad that You love us and that You are always with us. We know that nothing really bad can ever happen to us. Give us the Holy Spirit so that whenever we start being afraid, we will trust in You. Bless us and keep us, through Jesus Christ, our Savior. Amen.

Judge not, and you will not be judged. Luke 6:37

Little Lies and Big Harm

"Mother, Janey took my doll," said little Betty, with tears in her eyes. "She stealed it."

"Are you sure?" her mother asked.

"Uh-huh," she said. "We were sitting on a box under the porch. Now Janey is gone and my dolly is gone."

"Let's go look," said her mother. So together they went to the box under the porch and looked.

"Here is my doll," said Betty, and then she smiled at her mother.

But her mother didn't smile back.

"Betty, do you know you were a naughty girl just now?"

"How was I naughty, Mother?" she asked.

"You said a lie about Janey, didn't you?"

"You mean 'cause Janey *didn't* take my doll?" Betty asked.

"Yes, and if we wouldn't have looked, you would still be thinking a lie about Janey. Maybe you would be telling other people that Janey took your doll. Then they would think Janey steals."

"Would that be my fault, Mother?" asked Betty.

"Yes, it would be, honey," her mother told her. "Jesus calls it 'judging.' Jesus said, 'Judge not, and you will not be judged.' That means, 'Don't think and say mean things about other people.' When you talk about others, God will think you are bad, and so will people."

"I'm sorry," said Betty.

"I'm glad you're sorry," said her mother, "and glad that Jesus is willing to forgive you. Let's ask Him to keep you from ever doing it again, shall we?"

Betty nodded her head, and so they prayed together.

Some questions: What did Betty say about Janey? Where was the doll? What did Betty's mother say to her? How could Betty's words have hurt Janey? What did Jesus say in our Bible verse? What does this mean? Why did Jesus forgive Betty?

Bible reading: Luke 6:36-38.

Let us bow to pray: Dear Father in heaven, so very often we think and say bad things about others even when we don't have to. Please forgive us for Jesus' sake. Help us to remember how such words can hurt people, and give us the Holy Spirit so we will not want to do it. We ask this in Jesus' name. Amen.

*God called you by our
Gospel.* 2 Thessalonians 2:14

How God Calls

"Johnny! O Johnny!" Mrs. Nelson called. Johnny thought his mother wanted him to quit playing, so he hid behind the garage and didn't answer.

"Johnny, come right away!" his mother called again. His uncle wanted to take him along to the lake, but he was in a hurry. Because Johnny didn't come when he was called, he missed out on the trip. He was real sorry to hear about it later.

When God calls people and they don't even answer Him, they miss out on a lot more than a trip to a lake. They miss out on everything God wants to give them — forgiveness, happiness, a good life, a home in heaven.

How does God call people? The apostle Paul says in our Bible verse, *"God called you by our Gospel."* When ministers or Christian teachers or parents or anybody at all tell us that Jesus died for us and that God wants us to live with Him as His children, then God is calling us.

God is saying, "Johnny, Annie, Mary," or any other name in the world, "please come and be one of My children. I forgive you your sins because Jesus paid for them. I want you to have a home with Me in heaven and to enjoy My love on earth."

You'd think people would be glad to come and live with God when He calls, but many stay away from Him. They're afraid they may have to do something they don't want to do, or they think they have to stop having fun. But when they stay away from God, they miss the really great things they would enjoy, God's love and friendship.

We want God's love and forgiveness, His Holy Spirit, and His blessings. We want to live with Him and be with Him in heaven. That is why we come to Him when He calls us by the Gospel. The Gospel is the story of Jesus. The Gospel is His promise of love. With the good news that Jesus is our Savior God is calling us to live with Him forever.

Let's talk about this: Why didn't Johnny come when his mother called him? What did he miss by not answering her call? What does God want to give to all people? How does God call people to come to Him? Why don't all people come to God when He calls? How can we come to God every day?

Bible reading for older children and grownups: Isaiah 55:1-7.

Our prayer: Dear God, we thank You for calling us to enjoy all the good things You want to give to people. Please keep us from ever wanting to stay away from You, and give us Your love, through Jesus Christ, our Lord. Amen.

*Remember now your Creator in the days
of your youth.* Ecclesiastes 12:1

They Never Were Babies

"Mother," said Bobby, "why did God make Adam and Eve grown-up people? Why didn't they have to be babies like everybody else?"

Before his mother could answer, Freddy did. "How could they be babies?" he asked. "God would have had to make some other grownups to help the babies grow up."

Freddy was right. Babies need grownups. Most babies have a father and a mother. Those who do not have parents need someone else to love them and take care of them.

How does anybody get to be a good father or mother? Does that happen all at once when people get married? No, you are now becoming what you will be. The kind of boy or girl you are is the kind of father or mother you will probably be.

The boy who can't be sweet when things go wrong will be hard to live with when he is a father. The girl who is kind will probably be a kind mother, fun to live with, and sweet and helpful.

So ask God to help you put away bad temper and rough ways and mean words and selfish grabbing. The Bible says, "Remember now your Creator in the days of your youth." Then you will be a much better father or mother when you are big enough to get married and have children.

And the thing to remember most about God is the way He has loved you and loves you every day. God loved us and sent His Son to save us. By loving Jesus and living with Him in the days when you are young, you are more likely to be a Christian and a godly person when you are grown up.

90

Some questions to talk about: Which two people never were babies? Why didn't God make them as babies? What kind of parents do babies need? How can a child grow up to be a good father or mother? How can your father or mother help you to live with God in the days of your youth?

Bible reading for older children and grownups: Deuteronomy 6:4-7.

Let us pray: Thank You, dear heavenly Father, for a Christian home with family devotions, prayers, and other ways of remembering You and staying close to You. Help us to live with You now while we are young, so that we will be good Christian parents when we are grown up. We ask this for Jesus' sake. Amen.

Try to learn what is pleasing to the Lord. Ephesians 5:10

What Pleases the Lord Jesus?

"Find out what your mother would like for her birthday, will you, Jane?" said Mrs. Bart, the neighbor.

Jane was a clever girl. She talked to her mother about many different things, and never let her know why she was doing it.

The next day Jane told Mrs. Bart, "My mother would like a new coffee maker."

91

"Good girl," said Mrs. Bart. "I don't know how you ever found out."

"Oh, I found out by talking to her and getting her to talk to me," said Jane.

Some people say we can't find out what God would like to have from all of us. They think we can't know for sure what God wants and likes.

But we can, and we don't have to be any smarter than Jane. God was in the Lord Jesus. So we can learn to know God by learning to know Jesus.

And we can learn to know what Jesus would like to have from us. We can learn this by living with Him and talking with Him and letting Him tell us what pleases Him.

Jesus speaks to us in family devotions, in Bible reading, in Bible lessons, in church, and when we think about Him and have Him in our hearts. When we listen to Him often, we soon get to know pretty well what our Lord Jesus wants.

The apostle Paul said, "Try to learn what is pleasing to the Lord." We want to do that because we love Him. And we can. All we have to do is live with Him and listen to what He says.

Questions to help us think: How did Jane find out what would please her mother? How can we find out what is pleasing to Jesus? When does Jesus speak to us? When can we speak to Him? What does the Bible verse tell us to try to learn? Why do God's children want to learn what is pleasing to the Lord?

Bible reading for older children and grownups: Ephesians 5:8-14.

Let us bow to pray: Lord Jesus, please forgive us for often doing wrong and not doing what is pleasing to You. Please help us to know what the will of God is, and make us eager to do it all the time, for Your name's sake. Amen.

*How beautiful are the feet of those
who preach good news!* Romans 10:15

The Best Kind of Doctor

The Brown family was eating supper. Without anyone asking him, Johnny Brown said, "You know what I want to be when I grow up? I'm going to be a doctor."

"Why, that's fine, son," said Mr. Brown, rather surprised. "What made you decide to become a doctor?" he asked.

"Oh, doctors make lots of money," said Johnny.

"Is that the reason you want to be a doctor?" asked Johnny's mother. "I thought people became doctors because they wanted to help others," she said.

"Well, I guess that's a reason, too," Johnny said. "I'll bet I could help people more by being a doctor than any other way."

"Did you know that one of the writers of the Bible was a doctor?" asked Johnny's father.

"No. Who?" asked Johnny.

"Dr. Luke," his father told him. "The apostle Paul calls Luke 'the beloved doctor.'" Luke wrote the third book in the New Testament. He also wrote the book called "The Acts of the Apostles."

"Do you think Luke became a doctor because he wanted to help people?" asked Johnny.

"I don't know," said his father. "But I'm sure he wanted to help people *after* he knew Jesus. He helped their souls and their bodies."

"How'd he do that?" asked Johnny.

"He told people that Jesus was their Savior and Helper," said Johnny's father. "He taught them the way to life with God."

"Do you think I could be that kind of doctor?" asked Johnny.

"There are nurses and doctors doing that kind of work today. We call them medical missionaries. They go to faraway lands to heal people with medicine and also to tell them the good news about Jesus. But you wouldn't make nearly as much money as a regular doctor," his father told him.

"That's all right," said Johnny. "I'd like to be a medical missionary. Then I could help their souls *and* their bodies. Telling people about Jesus would help them even more than medicine."

Let's talk about this: What was Johnny Brown's first reason for wanting to become a doctor? What better reason did his mother give him? What is the name of the doctor who wrote two parts of the Bible? How did Dr. Luke help people's souls? What are doctors called when they are also missionaries for Jesus? Have you ever talked to God about what you might be?

Bible reading for older children and adults: Luke 10:1-9.

Our prayer: Dear Jesus, no matter what I may become, teach me to serve You by helping others. And don't let me forget to help others especially by telling them about You. Amen.

94

*The one who helps a prophet because he is a prophet
will get a prophet's reward.* Matthew 10:41

How Pengo Became a Prophet

Pengo couldn't talk very well. Most people couldn't
understand him. When he was born, the top of his mouth
wasn't right, and it never got any better.

Pengo lived in Africa, in a place where there was only
a witch doctor. The witch doctor couldn't help him. He
just frightened Pengo by telling him that devils kept him
from talking.

Then Pengo got smallpox. It left his face full of ugly
marks. Soon after that his parents died, and nobody wanted
Pengo. He had to live in a little grass hut by himself.

One day a missionary came and told about the love of
Jesus. Pengo had no one who loved him. So Pengo was
very glad to hear that Jesus loved him. He began to love
Jesus.

At first Pengo didn't tell anybody that he loved Jesus.
He thought they would laugh. He only told Jesus. At night,
when he was alone, he would say, "I'm so glad You love
me, Jesus. I'm so glad You died for me. I'm glad I belong
to You now. I will find some way to love You back."

So when the missionary needed a well, Pengo dug and
carried away the dirt until the well was deep enough and
the water came. When the missionary went on a trip, Pengo
went along and carried his things. When new missionaries
came, Pengo helped them by showing them where to go.

Pengo wished he could be a missionary, but missionaries
have to talk, and Pengo couldn't talk well. So he did what
he could, and it helped a lot.

Jesus will have a surprise for Pengo in heaven. In heaven

Pengo will be counted as a missionary. Jesus said, *"The one who helps a prophet because he is a prophet will get a prophet's reward."*

This means, "What we do for God's workers counts the same as what the workers do." When we help a minister do God's work, that's the same as being a minister.

Questions to talk about: Who was Pengo? What was his trouble? How did he get to know Jesus? What did he do for Jesus? Why did he help the missionaries? What surprise will Jesus have for him? How can we get a prophet's reward?

Bible reading: Matthew 10:38-42.

Our prayer: Dear Jesus, we don't deserve any pay or reward for what we do for You, but we are glad You have promised great blessings to all who help Your servants. Please make us willing to help anyone we can help, but especially the pastors and teachers and missionaries who work for You. Amen.

Look to Jesus, who . . .
  suffered on the cross. Hebrews 12:2

A Pretty Special Present

"Oh, boy! Today's my birthday," shouted Teddy as he got out of bed faster than usual.

Teddy could hardly wait to open his presents. You see, before leaving on a trip to Europe, Teddy's aunt had promised to send him something very special for his birthday, and the package had come the day before.

Teddy tore the wrappings from his aunt's package first. But when he saw what was in it, his mouth curled into a sour look. "Aw, it's only an old wooden cross," he said. "What good is that?"

Teddy's mother was sorry to hear what he said. "When we see a cross," she told him, "it reminds us of what Jesus did for us — that He died for us on a cross. All who believe that Jesus is their Savior receive the gift of life with God. That makes a cross something wonderful, doesn't it?"

Teddy was silent for a while. Then he said, "I can put it in my bedroom and look at it while I say my prayers. It will help me remember that Jesus died for me and that I belong to Him."

Now his mother was glad to hear what he said. The cross was a pretty special present after all.

"Look to Jesus, who . . . suffered on the cross," says the Bible. Jesus also tells us, "Anyone who does not take his cross and follow Me does not deserve Me."

The cross is both a reminder of what Jesus has done for us and what we ought to do for Him.

Let's talk about this: What did Teddy get from his aunt for his birthday? Why didn't Teddy like it at first? What did Teddy's mother tell him about the cross? Why does the Bible tell us to look to Jesus, who suffered on the cross? What are some things we ought to do for Jesus?

Bible reading for older children and adults: Matthew 10:37-42.

Our prayer: Dear Lord Jesus, whenever I see a cross, may it remind me of how You suffered and died for me, and help me to look to You for forgiveness and life with God. Amen.

The gift of God is eternal life through
Jesus Christ, our Lord. Romans 6:23

How Long Is Forever?

"Mother, how long is *forever?*" said little Mary. She was too small to know.

Her mother thought a minute. "It means always and always and always," she said.

"It means eternal, doesn't it, Mother?" said Verna, who was a little older and knew some big words.

"Yes," said her mother. "And the Bible tells us, 'The gift of God is eternal life through Jesus Christ, our Lord.' Jesus gives everlasting life — a life with God that will never end."

"Does that mean we'll be in heaven all the time when we die?" asked Mary.

"Yes," said her mother, "and we started to have that life when Jesus came into our hearts."

"But we're not in heaven already," said Verna. "Teacher said heaven is a place where people go when they die."

Then her mother explained that heaven is being with Jesus. "When He is in our hearts," she said, "we are in His kingdom on earth, and that's the beginning of heaven. Those who are His children when they die are taken to His kingdom in heaven."

"Does eternal life mean heaven?" asked Verna.

"Yes," said her mother. "And let's not forget to thank God for giving us this eternal life through Jesus Christ, our Lord. The Bible says, 'He who believes in the Son [of God] *has* everlasting life.'"

Questions to talk about: What does forever mean? What did Verna say it meant? When do people begin to have life with God? Why is heaven called eternal life? What did Verna's mother want her to remember?

Bible reading for grownups: Revelation 7:9-17.

Our prayer: Thank You, God, for giving us eternal life through Jesus Christ, our Lord. Keep us in His kingdom of heaven while we are living on earth so that we will be with Him in heaven forever after we die. We ask this in Jesus' name. Amen.

The wicked person borrows and never pays back. Psalm 37:21

Borrowing and Keeping

"How about letting me use your knife?" Charley asked his friend Eddie. "We're going camping this weekend, and I'll sure need one."

"Okay," agreed Eddie, "but bring it back to me Monday 'cause I need it for our club meeting."

"Sure thing," promised Charley. But when Eddie asked Charley for his knife at school the next Monday, Charley said he had forgotten to bring it along.

Every day Eddie asked Charley for his knife, and every day Charley said he forgot to bring it. Charley just didn't want to give back the knife.

Finally Eddie had to go over to Charley's house and make Charley give the knife back to him. He even had to tell Charley's mother. After that Charley and Eddie weren't good friends any more.

When someone is good enough to lend us something, we ought to remember that it's not ours "for keeps." When we're thankful to the person who is kind to us, we return what we borrow as soon as possible. The Bible says, "The wicked person borrows and never pays back."

It may not be easy to give back something that we like a lot, but God wants us to pay back what we borrow. It's not ours for keeps. Keeping is stealing. Stealing is a sin for which Jesus had to die. Remembering this will help us to give back what we borrow.

Let's talk about this: What does God's commandment say about stealing? What makes people want to steal? What does the Bible call a person who doesn't pay back what he borrows? What will we do if we love the person who lets us use something that belongs to him? Who takes away the sin of stealing and makes us want to return what we borrow?

Bible reading for older children and grownups: Ephesians 4:28-30.

Our prayer: Dear Jesus, please forgive the times we have wanted to steal or kept what did not belong to us. You gave Your life for us. Make us willing to give our hearts to You so that we will be glad to return to others what belongs to them. Amen.

God is Love. 1 John 4:8

Who Loves a Dirty Bum?

A nice man standing on a street corner handed Mary Jackson a little piece of paper. On one side of the paper was the picture of a bum, an ugly man. He hadn't shaved for a month, tobacco juice was in his beard, his hair wasn't combed, his vest didn't match his coat, and his shoes and pants were worn out.

Under the picture was the question "Who loves him?" On the back page were the words "Once he was some mother's darling." He probably was.

But who loves the bum now? As he walks down the street and begs dimes for another drink of whiskey, most people try not to look at him.

Who loves any person who isn't lovely? God does. The Bible says, "God is Love." He showed His love by sending His Son Jesus to pay for our sins.

The Bible also says, "God loved the world." That includes every person who ever lived in it or ever will live in it. "God so loved the world that He gave His only Son." In another place the Bible says, "Jesus died for all" in order to save all people from their sins.

Did Jesus die also for a bum? Jesus probably wouldn't call anyone a bum. Maybe we shouldn't either. But Jesus died for all, including bums. And even though He hates to see them be what they are, Jesus wants to save them and change them, too.

That's the wonderful thing about the love of God: We don't have to be rich or pretty or strong or important. We don't even have to be without sin. Anyone can have the love of God. All we need do is be sorry for our sins and believe in Jesus. God is Love!

Questions to talk about: What kind of picture was on the piece of paper a man handed to Mary Jackson? Who loves even a bum? What did Jesus do for all people? What ought we do also for bums because God loves us? Do we help a man by giving him money for whiskey? What is the best way to help a bum?

Bible reading for older children and grownups: 1 John 4:7-11.

Our prayer: Dear God, we thank You for sending Jesus to save all people, not just the good or the great or the lovely. Please help us to be more loving, more kind, more helpful, also to people who aren't lovely. For Jesus' sake we ask this. Amen.

God says, "He will call to Me,
and I will answer him." Psalm 91:15

When God Said No

Every night at the end of her prayers Dorothy said, "And please, God, let me have a bicycle for my birthday."

But Dorothy's parents were poor. Dorothy's daddy wanted very much to get her a bicycle, but when her birthday came, he still didn't have enough money.

Now her daddy worried that Dorothy might not trust God any more. She had prayed so long and hard for a bicycle. He was afraid that she might not love God if she didn't get a bicycle.

After Dorothy had opened her birthday presents, her daddy said, "Honey, I'm sorry you didn't get a bicycle. But don't blame God for not answering your prayers. I just didn't have enough money."

Dorothy said, "God answered my prayers, Daddy. He said, 'No; not yet.' He'll give you the money when He wants me to have a bike."

Dorothy's daddy was happy that his girl trusted God so well. He hugged her and held her close to him. She had taught him an important lesson about prayer.

Dorothy can teach us something about prayer, too. God doesn't always say "Yes" to our prayers. Some of the things we pray for might not be good for us. Because God loves us, He doesn't give us the things that may harm us.

God has three answers to prayers: Yes! No! Wait! God knows the best answer for us. Like Dorothy, we must believe that He loves us even when He says "No" or "Not yet."

God always listens to His children's prayers, and in the Bible He promises, "I will answer." He just doesn't always give us what we want when we want it.

Let's talk about this: For what did Dorothy pray every night before her birthday? Why was her daddy worried? What did Dorothy teach him about prayer? What does God promise to do when His children pray to Him? Why isn't His answer always "Yes"?

Bible reading for older children and adults: Psalm 91: 14-16.

Our prayer: Dear Father in heaven, help us to trust You as Dorothy did. Help us to believe that You always answer Your children when they pray to You. Teach us to be happy also when You say "No" or "Not yet," because You always love us so very much for Jesus' sake. Amen.

*A little with the fear of the Lord is better
than great treasure with trouble.* Proverbs 15:16

When a Little Is Better than Much

Once there was a mouse who lived out in the country where it wasn't always easy to find enough to eat. But there were no mousetraps in the field where the country mouse lived, so he was quite safe.

One day the country mouse visited his cousin in the city. While he was there, the city mouse showed him all the food in his house. There was a big cheese on the table, and butter, and sausage, and other foods that mice simply love to nibble at.

"I'd like to be a city mouse," said the country cousin. But just then a cat came into the room. "Hurry, run for the hole in the wall," said the city mouse. So they both ran for their lives. But in his hurry the city mouse ran right into a mousetrap, and "whang!" he was dead.

The country mouse got into the hole before the cat caught him. As soon as he had his breath back, he left the house with all the good eats and went back to the country. "I'd rather be safe than rich," he said.

Sometimes even Christians get jealous of rich people. But this is very foolish. The Bible says, "It is better to have just a little and a life with God than to have a lot and much trouble."

Jesus warned people about wanting to get rich. People who love money and lots of things often forget God. They easily lose their life with Him. The apostle Paul wrote: "Those who want to be rich easily fall into sin, into a trap, into many foolish and hurtful wishes."

The worst trouble anyone could have would come from losing life with Jesus. To have only a little and Jesus is much better than to be rich or famous without having His love and life with Him.

Questions to talk about: Where did the country mouse go for a visit? What happened to the rich city mouse? What did the poor country mouse decide? Why did Jesus warn us about wanting to get rich? What does our Bible verse say is better, a little with the Lord or a lot without Him?

Bible reading for older children and growups: Luke 12: 15-21.

Our prayer: Dear Father in heaven, You know what we need and what is best for us. Please give us only what is good for us and what we can use in helping other people. Keep us from ever wanting great riches without You. Remind us that it is much better to have just a little and life with You than a great treasure and much trouble. In Jesus' name we ask this. Amen.

Whatever you ask in prayer you will get,
if you have faith. Matthew 21:22

Learning to Pray

"Mommy, Mommy," cried Mary Jo as she came running up the front walk. Her mother hurried to the door and took the sobbing little girl into her arms.

"What's the matter, dear?" she asked.

"Oh, Mommy, Judy's awful sick, and an ambulance came and took her to the hospital," said Mary Jo. "Do you think she's going to die? Judy's my best friend, and I don't want her to die." Then Mary Jo began to cry harder than ever. Her mother tried to think of some way to comfort her.

"Isn't there anything we can do?" asked Mary Jo.

Then her mother thought of a way to help. "Dear," she said, "there is something we can do for Judy. We can pray. We can ask our Father in heaven to make Judy well. He loves Judy very much and knows what is best for her."

"Please pray to God right away, Mommy," begged Mary Jo.

But her mother said, "Since Judy is your best friend, don't you think you should be the one to ask God to help her?"

"What can I say?" asked Mary Jo.

"Just tell God what's the matter, the way you told me, and ask Him to help," said her mother.

So Mary Jo prayed. "Dear God," she said, "Judy, my best friend, is awful sick. I don't want her to die. Please make her well. Please do it for Jesus' sake. Amen."

Now Mary Jo felt better, and so did her mother. They believed that God would do what was best for Judy.

God loves us and will always answer our prayers if we

will trust Him. Jesus said, "Whatever you ask in prayer you will get, if you have faith."

So we needn't ever cry or worry about anything. All we need do is pray to God and trust Him. He loves us for Jesus' sake. When we belong to Jesus, our prayers are always answered in the best way — God's way.

Let's talk about this: What did Mary Jo's mother tell her she could do for her friend Judy? Why did Mary Jo feel better after she prayed? What does it mean to have faith? What did Jesus promise to all who trust Him? How do we know that God loves us and will do whatever is good for us?

Bible reading for older children and adults: John 15: 13-16.

Our prayer: Dear Jesus, please remind us to pray for whatever we need or want. Please also teach us to believe that whatever we ask in Your name we shall receive. Amen.

*The person with a cheerful heart
always has a good life.* Proverbs 15:15

The Secret of a Good Life

"There goes Bill, happy as ever," said Jim. "He's always cheerful. Nothing bothers him much."

"What makes you think nothing bothers him?" Jim's father asked.

"Oh, when we let him play in a game, he's happy. When we say he can't, he says, 'Okay, I'll watch.' When someone calls him a name, like 'Billy Goat,' he just grins and doesn't mind at all."

"Maybe he knows the secret of how to be happy," said Jim's father.

"I wish I could be that way," said Jim, whose feelings were easily hurt.

"You can be that way if you'll do what Bill does," said his father.

"What does Bill do?" asked Jim.

"Well," said his father, "Bill believes that God is always good to him, and he's thankful for what he gets from God and never complains."

"So that's how he carries his fun around inside of him," said Jim. "I'm going to ask God to make *me* that way."

"That's a good idea," said Jim's father. "The Bible says, 'The person with a cheerful heart always has a good life.' We can have a cheerful heart because Jesus gives us God's love."

So the secret of a good life is to keep Jesus in your heart and to remember the many blessings God gives you.

Let's talk about this: Why was Bill always cheerful? What did Jim decide to ask God? How did God show that He loves us? How can every one of us have a cheerful heart? Why can we always be happy with Jesus? Who can say the Bible verse from memory?

Bible reading for older children and grownups: Psalm 103:1-13.

Our prayer: Lord God, help us to feel thankful that we have You as our Father and Jesus as our Savior. Give us the Holy Spirit so that we will always be cheerful, through Jesus Christ, our Lord. Amen.

You must help us by prayer. 2 Corinthians 1:11

Each Night at Six

"We wish we could go with you," said some of the young people to the missionary who had talked to their Sunday school. The missionary was leaving to work for Jesus in a country across the ocean.

"Come with me in your prayers every day," said the young missionary. "You can help me by praying for me."

"We could all promise to pray for you every evening at six o'clock," said a girl in the group. And that is what some of them decided to do. Each night at six o'clock they prayed for the young missionary and his work.

Our prayers do great things for the people who work for God, because God gladly listens to those prayers. The Bible says, "The prayer of a righteous man has great power."

The apostle Paul wanted his friends to pray for him. When he wrote to them, he said, "You must help us by prayer so that many people will thank God for the blessings given to us in answer to many prayers."

Our missionaries today also say, "You must help us by prayer." Our pastors and our teachers in the church say, "You must help us by prayer." All the other people who work for Jesus in His church say, "You must help us by prayer."

We could write a list of people to pray for. It would help us remember certain missionaries and other servants of Jesus. Let us pray for these people each night at a certain time. Remember, they are doing their work also for us, and we can help them by our prayers.

Let's think about this: What did some young people wish they could do? What did the missionary tell them?

How did the young people help the missionary? What reason did the apostle Paul give his friends for praying? Who are some of the people we could help by prayer?

Bible reading: 2 Corinthians 1:8-11.

Let us pray: Dear Father in heaven, please remind us to pray often for Your missionaries and other workers. Today we ask You to bless especially (here name the people for whom you wish to pray) and their work for You. In Jesus' name we ask it. Amen.

Jesus came into the world to save sinners. 1 Timothy 1:15

Our Lord's Big Job

"Mother, why don't pictures ever show Jesus smiling?" asked Jimmy.

His mother thought a moment and then answered, "Well, Jimmy, not all pictures show Him looking serious. I remember a picture of Jesus smiling," she said. "He was listening to some children praise Him in the temple, and He was smiling."

"That was on my Sunday school paper," said Jimmy. "But why do *most* pictures of Jesus show Him looking real serious?" he asked.

110

"Well," said his mother, "did you ever notice how serious the rulers of countries usually look in their pictures?"

"Sure, that's because they have a big job to do," said Jimmy.

Jimmy's mother nodded and said, "Yes, Jimmy, and Jesus had a much bigger job to do than any president or king. Jesus had the work of saving the whole world from sin and from the punishment of sin. He even had to die to finish the work."

Jimmy thought about this awhile, and then he said, "I guess it's a good thing that Jesus looks serious in His pictures. They remind us of the important work He did."

"Yes," said his mother. "And let's not forget that He did it for us. The Bible says, 'Jesus came into the world to save sinners,' and that includes us. But do you know something else?"

"What?" asked Jimmy.

"I'm sure Jesus smiled often when He was with His friends."

"I think so, too," said Jimmy. "Anyone who loves people smiles at them."

Let's talk about this: Why do most pictures of Jesus show Him looking serious? What does our Bible verse say Jesus came to do? Who are the people called sinners? What did Jesus do to save us? How can we be saved from our sins? Why did Jimmy think Jesus smiled often?

Bible reading for older children and grownups: 1 Timothy 2:1-6.

Our prayer: Dear Jesus, thank You for coming into the world to save sinners. Thank You also for saving us by coming into our hearts. Make us friendly, and give us a bright smile because we belong to You and receive Your love every day. Amen.

Let all . . . evil speaking
be put away. Ephesians 4:31

Unkind Words

"That Sue! She's always getting hundreds on her tests. I'll bet she cheats," Ann complained to some of her friends. Soon the friends were whispering that Sue got good grades because she cheated.

Ann knew that Sue didn't cheat. She knew that Sue studied hard to get good grades. But Ann was jealous. Ann's mother was always asking her why she couldn't be like Sue. This was Ann's way of getting even with Sue.

Because of what Ann said, the girls in the class soon didn't talk friendly to Sue any more. They gave her mean looks and said mean things about her. This made Sue feel very sad. She didn't even want to go to school any more.

When Ann saw what her unkind words had done to Sue, she began to feel bad about it. She tried to tell the other girls that Sue didn't really cheat. But some of the girls kept on saying bad things about Sue anyway.

At last Sue's mother and father decided they must move so that Sue could go to a different school. Their Sue wasn't ever happy any more because her heart was sick. So they moved away, all because a girl was jealous and had said some mean lies.

When you are tempted to say mean things about someone, remember the commandment of God which says, "Thou shalt not bear false witness against thy neighbor." Do you know what that means?

Martin Luther explained it this way: "We should love God so much that we will not purposely tell lies about anyone, nor mention his mistakes, nor talk about him behind his back, nor spread harmful stories about him. But we should defend our neighbor and say the best we can about him."

Jesus died to save us also from the sin of unkind words. To His children He says, "Let all . . . evil speaking be put away." Loving Jesus and people helps us to put all evil speaking away.

Let's talk about this: What unkind words did Ann say about Sue? Why was this wrong? What harm did Ann's words do? Can you say God's commandment against lying? What does this commandment mean? What does our Bible verse says about evil speaking? Let's see how long we can keep from saying anything bad about another person.

Bible reading for older children and grownups: 1 Peter 3:10-12.

Our prayer: Dear Jesus, please take away all evil speaking from out of our mouths. Give us the Holy Spirit so that we will speak only what is good and helpful to others. Amen.

*Give to God the things
that are God's.* Mark 12:17

Don't Steal from God

Two girls saw a little neighbor girl on the back steps of her house. She was playing with a lovely doll. She was dressing it first with one pretty outfit and then with another.

"May we play with you?" asked the two big girls. The little girl was pleased and said they could. But then the two big girls took the doll and the doll clothes and wouldn't let the little girl have them back for a long time, not even when she cried.

What do you think of those older girls? They weren't fair to the little girl, were they?

Some people treat God that way. They take God's things and act as though His things belonged to them. They use His gifts just for themselves and don't give anything back to God.

What belongs to God? Well, everything does. Our life comes from God and belongs to Him. Our time, our money, our family, our home, our mind — all our blessings are given to us by God. He wants us to use them to help other people.

Mr. Brown believed that everything he had really belonged to God and that God was just letting him use His things for a while. He also loved God for sending His Son Jesus to die for all of us. So Mr. Brown worked for God by giving God a part of all the money he received. He also used his car to bring people to Sunday school and church meetings, and gave God some of his time every day.

Do you know what God wants from us more than anything else? He wants our heart, our love. Jesus said, "The first and great commandment is this: You must love the

Lord, your God, with all your heart." The more we do this, the easier it will be to give God the things that are God's.

Questions to talk about: Why was it wrong for the girls to play with the doll by themselves? What things do we have that belong to God? How do some people keep God's things away from Him? How did Mr. Brown use his car for God? What does God want more than anything else? Why do Christians give God their love?

Bible reading: Malachi 3:7-10.

Let us bow and pray: Dear God, we thank You for the many things You have given us to use for a while. Please help us to remember that they really belong to You so that we will use them in Your ways and for Your work. In Jesus' name we ask this. Amen.

Jesus said, *"I stand at the door and knock."* Revelation 3:20

Letting Jesus into Our Hearts

"Here, Billy, please take this ice cream to your sisters," said his mother. She was dishing out a quart his father had brought home. So Billy took two servings up the stairs to where his sisters were playing.

"Let's not let Billy in," said his sisters when they heard him coming. They quickly locked the door to their room. When Billy knocked on the door and called to them, the

115

sisters wouldn't open the door. They didn't know he was bringing them ice cream.

At last Billy went back down to the kitchen. "They wouldn't open the door," Billy told his mother.

"Well, then, we'll eat as much as we want, and we'll put the rest away," said his father. "They'll not get any until they're sorry about the way they acted."

The sisters were foolish for being mean to their brother. But there are many people who are much more foolish. Somebody is always knocking at their door and wants to give them something much better than ice cream.

Jesus says, "Look, I stand at the door and knock." He means that He wants to come into our hearts. He wants to give us His love and life with God. He said, "If anyone hears My voice and opens the door, I will come in to him and eat with him and he with Me."

But some people don't open the door. They don't let Him in. They never say, "Come in, Lord Jesus." Even though He's like a brother to us, we sometimes don't let Him give us His love either. When we quarrel or lie or are mean, we are shutting our hearts to Jesus. Then we miss out on what God wants to give us. People who keep Him out altogether even miss out on heaven.

Let's talk about this: What did the mother want to give Billy's sisters? Why did they lock their door? Why were they foolish in doing so? What did Jesus say in our Bible verse? At what kind of door is He always knocking? How do we let Him in?

Bible reading: Revelation 3:15-20.

Let us pray: Dear Jesus, thank You for calling to us and wanting to give us the blessings of God and of heaven. Please live in our hearts every day, and give us forgiveness of sins and a new spirit. Keep us from ever refusing to open the door of our hearts to You, our Lord and Savior. Amen.

*Let your light so shine that people may see your good works
and will praise your Father who is in heaven.* Matthew 5:16

Where Good Baby Sitters Come from

"Those baby sitters from Grace Church are the best you can get," Mrs. Brant told Mrs. Grey. "Last night we had our third one, and they're just grand."

"Who are they?" asked Mrs. Grey.

"Oh, they're a club of teen-agers who took lessons in baby-sitting at their church. They try to do the job for God as well as they can. They're kind and play with the children. They tell Bible stories. They remind the children to pray, and they try to teach the children good behavior."

"Well, the Lord knows my children need that," said Mrs. Grey.

"Our children love them," said Mrs. Brant. "I wouldn't get anyone else. These young people are sweet and good. You can tell that they love God in what they do. They aren't just trying to earn money."

"Well," said Mrs. Grey, "they certainly are letting their faith shine."

"Yes, they are," said Mrs. Brant. "I hope my children will grow up like that with God in their hearts. It's wonderful what God can do to any person who loves Jesus."

Those two mothers were praising our Father in heaven for what those teen-age baby sitters did. Jesus wants us all to do kind and good things for other people so that they will see how wonderful God is. That's why He said, "Let your light so shine that people may see your good works and will praise your Father who is in heaven."

When we do kind things for other people and things that are good, then people can see how wonderfully well God can change a person and how good it is to have His love. This may also lead them to want Jesus in their hearts, that they, too, can be God's children. So let your light shine.

Questions to talk about: Why did Mrs. Brant like the baby sitters from Grace Church? What helped them do their job well? Why did Mrs. Grey praise God? What did Jesus say we should let people see? Why? What is our light? How can we let our light shine?

Bible reading: Matthew 5:13-16.

Let us pray: Dear Father in heaven, please help us to let the light of our faith in Jesus shine in whatever we do. Make us more loving, more helpful, more kind, so that people will praise You for what we do, through Jesus Christ, our Lord. Amen.

*Children, obey your parents
in all things.* Colossians 3:20

Who Knows What's Best?

"Aw, Mom, why can't I go over to Tommy's house?" asked Dick. His mother answered, "You know that Tommy is always getting into trouble."

But Dick argued with his mother. "He never does anything bad when I'm with him. Please, Mom, Tommy's O. K. Why can't I go?"

His mother said, "I'm sorry, Dick, but I think it would be better if you didn't go over to Tommy's house. I've tried to explain why. You'll have to believe that I know what's best."

But Dick thought he knew better. So he got very angry and wouldn't eat any supper. He just sat around grumbling. "My mom's old-fashioned," he was thinking to himself. "Tommy's a good guy. Boy, I'll bet I'm missing all kinds of fun tonight."

Later that evening the telephone rang. It was Dick's friend Jack. "Hey, Dick, did you hear what happened to Tommy tonight?" said Jack. "He was caught trying to steal something in a store."

As Dick hung up the phone, he said to himself, "Wow! Tommy's in jail. Boy, am I glad I wasn't with him tonight! Lucky for me Mom made me stay home." So Dick learned that parents usually do know what's best.

In the Bible God says, "Children, obey your parents in the Lord, for this is right." God knows what's best. That's why He says in another place, "Children, obey your parents in all things, for this is well pleasing to the Lord."

The Lord Jesus wants His children to obey their parents.

119

Those who do so out of love for Jesus please Him. Are you always willing to please Jesus?

Let's talk about this: Why did Dick grumble and refuse to eat his supper? How did Dick learn that his mother was right? What does God say about children obeying parents? Why are Christian children willing to obey their parents? Let's say the Bible verse together.

Bible reading for older children and grownups: Proverbs 1:7-15.

Our prayer: Lord Jesus, teach me to gladly obey my parents, especially in all things that are pleasing to You. Amen.

*By breaking the Law
you dishonor God.* Romans 2:23

Wearing the Uniform of Christ

Bob's dad was admiring his son's new jacket. It had the name of their church across the back. Bob was on the church basketball team for boys.

"Mr. Evans told us to take off the jacket whenever we don't act like a Christian," said Bob. Mr. Evans was the team's coach. He wanted to be sure that the team didn't disgrace God or His church.

Bob's dad said, "I think that's a good way of putting it. If people would see you do something wrong in your church uniform, they might think less of God."

And that's true. The Bible says to God's people, "By breaking the Law you dishonor God." In a way every Christian wears God's uniform as long as he calls himself a Christian. When a Christian does something wrong, people do

120

not just say, "Look at what he does." They often say, "That's what a Christian does!"

On the other hand, when we're honest and polite and friendly and helpful and cheerful, people also see that. Then they may not only say, "That Bob is the nicest boy." We hope they will also say, "Christians are good people. They're different. I wonder why. I'd like to be one."

People who love God don't want to dishonor and disgrace Him by breaking His laws. The love of Jesus keeps them from doing so. He forgives them when they sin and are sorry, and He gives them the Holy Spirit. The Holy Spirit makes them the kind of children God can be proud of.

Let's talk about this: What kind of jacket was Bob wearing? Why did his coach tell him to take off the jacket if he ever wanted to do something wrong? What does the Bible say happens whenever God's children break His laws? What are some of His laws? Why is God disgraced when Christians break His laws? How does Jesus help His people?

Bible reading for older children and grownups: Romans 2:21-24.

Let us bow to pray: Heavenly Father, please forgive us for Jesus' sake if we have ever shamed You before others. Give us the Holy Spirit so that Your name will be honored in all that we do. In Jesus' name we ask this. Amen.

*Ask, and God will give it
to you.* Matthew 7:7

A Right Way to Ask

"Bread!" shouted Gene. But nobody at the table paid any attention to him. Before Gene had come to the table, his family had decided to teach him to say "please."

"Bread!" said Gene loudly again, but nobody passed the bread.

"Bread!" he said still louder, but he didn't get any bread that way.

"Will somebody please give me a piece of bread?" he finally asked in a polite way. Then everybody tried to give him bread at once.

"Oh, I get it!" he said. "You're trying to teach me to say 'please.'"

In a few days Gene learned to ask for things politely. He found out that saying "please" works much better than shouting and demanding.

God, too, likes to be asked instead of told. When people act as though God owed them things, they can't expect God to listen to them. When people get angry because God doesn't give them what they want, they forget that they deserve nothing but punishment from God because they often break His laws.

"Ask, and God will give it to you," said Jesus. But we must believe God and ask in a right spirit. "Whatever you

122

ask in prayer, you will receive," said Jesus, "if you have faith."

What does it mean to have faith? It means believing that God loves us for Jesus' sake, that He is our Father, that He is almighty and can answer any prayer, that He is good and wants to give us only that which is good for us. To have faith in God is to trust God.

Anyone who has faith in God will ask Him for many things, but will always ask politely. He will not treat God like a waiter. He will not ask for things he wants as though God owed them to him. No, he will trust that God will answer prayers because He is kind and good.

Let's talk about this: Why didn't Gene get the bread he wanted? What did he learn from his family? What did Jesus say about asking God for things? Does God give us what we ask because we are good or because He is good? What are some wrong ways of asking? What does it mean to have faith? How are we to ask God for things?

Bible reading about prayer: Luke 11:5-13.

Our prayer: Dear Father in heaven, please give us the Holy Spirit so that we will ask You for right things in a right way, through Jesus Christ, our Lord. Amen.

Every good athlete practices self-control
in all things. 1 Corinthians 9:25

How to Be a Good Athlete

At the supper table one evening Jim said, "Dick Maze is the fastest runner in the world, and he never smokes or drinks whiskey or even coffee."

"And he always gets plenty of sleep," his mother added because Jim never wanted to go to bed.

"I want to be a good athlete if I can't be a minister," said Jim.

"To be a good athlete you have to practice every day," said his dad.

"Sure, it's like playing the piano," said his sister Nancy. "Sometimes I get so tired of practicing. But now I like it better, because I can play pieces."

"It takes hard work to be good in anything," said Jim's mother. "Even being a good Christian takes practice."

"We talked about that at church one day," said Jim. "In the Bible the apostle Paul tells us to be sure to win our race. He meant our race to heaven."

"Yes," said his dad, "and do you remember what St. Paul said every good athlete does? 'Every good athlete practices self-control in all things.' What do you think that means?"

Jim thought it meant taking good care of his body.

"Right," said his dad. "St. Paul tells us that athletes take care of their bodies to win a prize which isn't worth much, but we do it for God."

"Like eating what is good for us and not eating too much and not smoking if it hurts our health and not getting drunk?" asked Jim.

"Yes," said his mother. "It also means training our bodies

124

to do the things God wants us to do, like helping people and being polite and friendly and smiling and praying and going to church and saying 'No' to sin."

"Does that take practice, too?" asked Jim.

"It certainly does," said his mother. "And it helps to make us strong Christians so that we can win our race to heaven."

Let's talk about this: How did the good runner try to keep himself strong? Why did he do this? What did Saint Paul say every good athlete does? What can we do to help us win our race to heaven?

Bible reading about athletes: 1 Corinthians 9:24-27.

Our prayer: Heavenly Father, please help us to avoid everything that might keep us from being good Christians, and lead us to do everything that will help us to win our race to heaven. We ask this in the name of Jesus, who died to save us. Amen.

God the Father said, "Jesus is My dear Son; listen to Him." Mark 9:7

Better Listen to Jesus

"Better take your raincoat along, Bob," said his mother. "It looks like rain."

"Aw, Mom, you're always afraid of rain," said Bob. "It won't rain."

When Bob came home, he was wet to the skin. His suit was soaked, and he was shivering. For three days after that he had a very bad cold.

It would be better for Bob if he learned to listen to his mother. God wants children to obey their parents. Those who do so are blessed, and those who don't usually suffer in one way or another.

But there is a worse kind of not listening. God the Father said several times in the Bible, "Jesus is My dear Son; listen to Him." When people don't listen to Jesus, they get into trouble with God.

Jesus says He is our Savior. He said that all people are lost sinners and that He came to save them. He said He is the Good Shepherd, who gave His life for His sheep. People ought to listen when He says who He is.

Jesus also says in the Bible that we need His forgiveness every day because we daily do many wrong things. But some people don't believe Jesus. They think they're all right the way they are. They don't listen to Him.

Jesus said, "Come to Me, everyone who has a load on his mind and heart, everyone who has worries and troubles, and I will give you rest." Jesus said this because He loves us and wants to help us. But many people don't listen, and then they don't get the love of Jesus.

Jesus also wants us to obey His teachings. To His followers He said, "If a man love Me, he will keep My words, and My Father will love Him, and We will come to him and live with him."

God the Father wants us to listen to Jesus, because Jesus can save us and bless us. He wants to give us God's forgiveness and love and a wonderful life with God and a home in heaven. The more we listen to Him, the better.

Let's talk about this: What happened to Bob because he didn't listen to his mother? Who said that all people should listen to Jesus? Why should we listen to Jesus? What are some of the things Jesus has said? What do people get when they listen to Jesus? What happens when people don't listen to Jesus?

Bible reading: Mark 9:2-7.

Let us pray: Dear God, our Father in heaven, please make us willing to listen to Jesus at all times. Help us to believe that Jesus is our Savior so that we will receive the life You want to give us through Him. In Jesus' name we ask it. Amen.

You don't have because you don't ask. James 4:2

You Can Keep On Asking God

Bob and Betty went to a skating rink with two friends. But the place was closed up. The man who was sweeping the entrance said, "It won't be open until tomorrow."

The friends turned around and went home. But Bob and Betty hung around a while longer. "How about letting us skate just a little while?" Betty asked the man. "We'll try not to get in your way, if you'll let us in."

"Well, all right," said the man. So Betty and Bob got in because they asked. Their friends missed out on the skating.

God wants us to ask Him for what we want. Even if it is something we think we can never have, God wants us to ask for it. He says, "You don't have because you don't ask." In another place Jesus said, "Ask, and God will give it to you"; that is, of course, if it is good for us.

God even wants us to *keep on* asking if our prayers aren't answered right away. It isn't right to pester *people.* It isn't right to whine and pout for something when our *parents* have said "No." But *God* wants us to keep on asking Him for what we want or need.

Jesus once told a story about a man who got some company late one night. The company was hungry, but he didn't have any bread to serve. So the man went to his neighbor's house to borrow some bread and pounded on the door.

At first the friend looked out of an upstairs window and said, "Don't bother me now. My children and I are already in bed." But when the man kept on asking, his friend got up and gave him what he wanted.

When Jesus finished telling this story, He said, "In the same way keep on asking God for what you want."

Let's talk about this: How did Betty and Bob get into the skating rink? Why didn't their friends get in? Why is it wrong to pester people? What story did Jesus once tell? Why did Jesus tell that story? What does the Bible verse say? What does it teach us?

Bible reading: Luke 11:5-10.

Let us pray: Dear heavenly Father, we are glad that You want us to ask You for whatever we want. Please teach us to pray more than we do, and help us to remember Your promise to give us what is good for us if we will ask You for it. In Jesus' name we ask this. Amen.

*From within, out of the heart,
come evil thoughts.* Mark 7:21

Where the Trouble Lies

One day when George was home alone, he dropped the kitchen clock. After that the hands wouldn't run right, so he took the glass off and ran with the hands to the watch shop nearby.

"Please fix these hands right away," he said to the watch repair man.

The man laughed and said, "The hands are all right. If you want me to fix the clock, you'll have to bring me the *inside* of the clock."

"But the hands aren't going right," explained George.

"I know," said the man. "But that's because there's something wrong *inside* the clock."

When *your* hands go wrong, do you know that the trouble is inside you? If your hands pull somebody's hair or steal or fight or do other wrong things, putting medicine on the hands won't make them better.

To fix what your hands do, God has to fix your heart or spirit, which is on the inside. Jesus said, "From within, out of the heart, come evil thoughts." First we think wrong, and then we do wrong.

God fixes us on the inside by giving us the Holy Spirit when we come to Jesus for fixing. The Holy Spirit gives us a new heart, a heart that loves Jesus, our Savior, and wants to be like Him. God does this fixing free of charge as often as we come to Him. And when He fixes us on the inside, then our hands go right, and our whole behavior gets straightened out, too.

Let's think about this: What did George want the watch repair man to do? Why couldn't the man fix the hands? When our hands go wrong, what needs fixing? What did Jesus say about this? How can we get our hands fixed?

Bible reading for grownups: Mark 7:14-23.

Our prayer: Please give us a new, clean heart, O God, and a right spirit inside us. Forgive us our sins for Jesus' sake, and help us to think His way so that we will then also walk in His ways. Amen.

When I am weak,
then I am strong. 2 Corinthians 12:10

Weak but Mighty

Pastor Jacobs wanted Jane's father to be a Sunday school teacher.

"I can't teach," he said. "I don't know my Bible well enough. I don't know how to handle children. And I never went to college. You better get somebody else who would be better than I."

"What's this lying here?" asked Pastor Jacobs.

"A pencil," answered Jane's father, wondering what Pastor Jacobs had in mind.

"What can a pencil do by itself?" asked Pastor Jacobs.

130

"It can't do anything by itself," said Jane's father. He smiled as he began to see what was coming. "It depends on who holds the pencil and what he does with it."

"I see," said the pastor. "Are you like a pencil that hasn't been sharpened, or are you a pencil that God couldn't use?"

"Oh, I'm sure God could do something with me if He took hold of me," said Jane's father, laughing at himself.

"Well, then," said the pastor, "why don't you let Him use you as a teacher? Our Sunday school needs teachers, and the children and young people in our Sunday school need teachers."

"But aren't there some better people God could use?" Jane's father still argued.

"Perhaps," said the pastor, "but God told the apostle Paul, 'My power is made perfect in weakness.' That's why Paul said, 'For the sake of Christ, then, I am satisfied with weaknesses . . . for when I am weak, then I am strong.' Christians who know how weak they are, are the strongest when they ask God to make them strong."

Well, after that Jane's father decided to join the Sunday school teacher-training class. And when he told God that he was weak and asked God to help him become a good teacher, God made him strong.

Questions to talk about: What was Jane's father asked to do? Why didn't he want to? Who are the strongest Christians? Why are we strong only when we know we are weak? Why was the apostle Paul satisfied to be weak? What did Jane's father decide to do?

Bible reading: 2 Corinthians 12:7-10.

Let us pray: Dear Lord, we are small and weak in Your kingdom, and we can do nothing without Your power. Help us to remember that we are weak so that we will let You do mighty and great things through us. In Jesus' name we ask it. Amen.

The Best Fighting System

Bob came home full of pep after having gym at school.

"We're learning self-defense," he said. "We're learning the Sullivan System."

"What's the Sullivan System?" his mother asked.

"It's hitting the other fellow before he can hurt you," said Bob.

"What do you think of the *Solomon* System?" his mother asked.

"The Solomon System?" said Bob. "I never heard of it."

"It's the best system in the world," said his mother.

"What's it like, Mom?" he asked.

"You'll find it in Proverbs 15:1," she answered, pointing to a Bible on the table.

"In the Bible?" asked Bob, as if it couldn't be true.

"Look it up for yourself," she said, so he did. It said, "A soft answer turns away anger."

"I get it," said Bob. "Bill did that when Joe was mad and wanted to fight him."

"What did Bill say?" Bob's mother asked.

He said, "I'm sorry, Joe, I'd rather be your friend."

"What happened?"

"Well," said Bob, "it took the wind right out of Joe's blowing, and there just was no fight."

"Isn't that the surest way to win a fight?" his mother asked. "That's the way Jesus won many of *His* fights with *His* enemies."

Let's talk about this: What was Bob learning in gym? What system did Solomon teach? Where did Bob find the

Solomon System? Why is a soft answer a good way to win a fight? How does Jesus help us to give soft answers?

Bible reading: Proverbs 15:1-4.

Let us pray: Father in heaven, we have such sharp tongues, and we are so quick to say mean things. Please forgive us. Make us more loving so that we will give soft answers and may win fights by making peace, as Jesus would. In His name we ask this. Amen.

Jesus said, "If anyone hits you on the right cheek, turn to him the left one also." Matthew 5:39

Why Not Hit Back?

"Charles, why did you push Ann?" his mother asked him sadly.

" 'Cause she pushed me first," said Charles, thinking he had a right to do the same.

"What do you think Jesus would have done, Charles, if He had been pushed?" his mother asked him.

"He would have — I don't know what He would have done," Charles answered.

"I know what He said about hitting back," his mother told him. "Get your Bible, Charles, and find Matthew 5, verse 39."

Charles brought his Bible to her, and together they found the verse. In it Jesus said, "If anyone hits you on the right cheek, turn to him the left one also."

"Would Jesus have said, 'You may push Me again'?" asked Charles.

"That's what it sounds like to me," said his mother. "At least He wouldn't have pushed back."

Does this mean that God's children must let people push them and hit them? No, everyone has a right to protect himself. But Jesus meant that it's better to be hurt than to hurt somebody. He wants us to love even those who hurt us. And He would rather that we let someone hurt us a second time than that we get angry and hit back.

Jesus let people hurt Him and even kill Him to save them from their sins. He saved us, too. When Jesus is in our hearts, we can keep from hitting and hurting others even when they push us.

Let's talk about this: What wrong did Ann do? What did Charles think he had a right to do? What do you think Jesus probably did when someone pushed Him? What did Jesus say about hitting back? Why ought we to be willing to forgive people who hurt us? How can we become willing?

Bible reading: Matthew 5:38-42.

Let us pray: Dear Father in heaven, we often get angry and want to hit back. Please forgive also this sin for Jesus' sake. Help us to be kind and good, as You are. In Jesus' name we ask this. Amen.

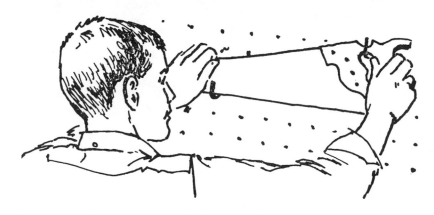

He who is faithful in small things is faithful
also in big things; and he who cheats in little things
also cheats in big things. Luke 16:10

What Small Things Tell

A businessman who became rich always watched his new workers carefully.

One day he hired a boy to sweep and clean in his factory. Then he said to the boy's boss, "Let the boy do as he likes, but tell me what he does with his time and with his things."

After a week the boss of the factory told the owner, "The boy does his work well and takes good care of the things he works with."

The owner was glad to hear this, but he decided to see for himself. Just before the boy came to work the next day, he threw a clean rag on the floor, and laid a saw on some nails, where it could easily be scratched. Then he watched.

When the boy came by, he picked up the rag, shook it out, and laid it with his other clean rags. Then he picked up the saw and hung it on the wall where it belonged.

When the owner saw that the boy was careful and faithful in little things, he said to the boy, "How would you like

135

a job in our office? If you will keep on doing your work well, we'll make you a manager someday."

This businessman could guess that the boy would be a good worker. He could tell by watching how he did his little jobs while he was young.

We can guess how good a father a boy will be by what he does now; or how good a mother a girl will be by what she does now. The little things we do, even when we are little, tell the story of how well we will probably do big things when we are bigger.

That's part of what Jesus meant when He said, "He who is faithful in small things is faithful also in big things; and he who cheats in little things also cheats in big things."

Questions to talk about: What did the businessman ask the boss of his factory to watch? Why did he throw a clean rag on the floor? How did the boy show he could be trusted to do his work well? How can we tell what kind of father or mother a boy or girl will be? How can we know what kind of worker we'll be in a big job?

Bible reading: Luke 16:10-13.

Our prayer: Heavenly Father, please help us do our work and even little things in such a way that we will grow up to be good parents and good workers for our Lord Jesus. In His name we ask this. Amen.

Salvation comes from the Jews. John 4:22

Why Christians Love Jews

Don and his family lived next door to a family of Jews. They were good neighbors, and he and young Manie were friends.

One day the house on the other side of Don's house was sold. It was bought by another Jewish man for him and his family.

"Aren't you afraid to live between Jews?" George asked Don when he heard that Don's new neighbors were Jews.

"Why should I be?" asked Don. "Manie is one of my best friends, and he's a Jew. His parents are good to me, too. They're nicer than some of our other neighbors."

"Yeah, but some people don't like Jews," said George.

"They just don't know any better," said Don. "All the men except Luke, who wrote the Bible, were Jews. Even Jesus was a Jew, and Mary was, and Samuel, and Moses. Some of the greatest and best men who ever lived were Jews."

"But don't forget that Jews killed Jesus, and some of them cheat people," said George. He had heard his father say that.

"My dad says that's a reason for loving them," said Don. "The enemies of Jesus killed Him long ago because they didn't know who He was and how He loved them. But the closest friends of Jesus and the first Christians were Jews."

Jesus once said, "Salvation comes from the Jews." Jesus came from the Jewish people. By living and dying for us, He saved us from our sins and from God's punishment of our sins. The Bible, which tells us about this salvation, also came from Jews.

So we, too, can say that salvation comes from the Jews. For this we ought to love them and try to lead them to love Jesus, too.

Some questions: What kind of people lived next to Don's house? Why was George worried? What did Don tell George? What did Jesus say comes from the Jewish people? How did salvation come to us from the Jews? What special reason do Christians have for loving Jews?

Bible reading for grownups: Romans 3:1-3, 9, 28-30.

Our prayer: Dear Father in heaven, thank You for giving us the Bible and Jesus and all Your promises of love and salvation through the Jewish people. Please lead many Jews to believe in Jesus, and help us to show Your love to them by the way we treat them. For Jesus' sake we ask it. Amen.

Let no one say when he is tempted,
"I am tempted by God." James 1:13

The Moths That Got Burned

It was nighttime. Tom and Sally were watching a big moth flying around the street light in front of their house. The moth often hit his head hard against the hot glass.

But that didn't stop him from flying at it. He wanted to get into the light.

A few days later a man came by to clean the lamp. When he took the shade off, about a dozen dead moths fell from the top. They had died trying to get into the light. The light had burned them.

"You know what this reminds me of?" said the caretaker to Tom, who was standing nearby and watching. "It reminds me of how we often want something that isn't good for us, and how we get hurt when we follow our temptations."

"But a moth can't help wanting to get to the light, can it?" asked Tom.

"Well, no," said the man. "And in a way we're as helpless as a moth. We can't keep ourselves from being tempted to sin. The bad wishes are in us. But we can't blame God for that. He didn't make us that way. The Bible says, 'God tempts no one, but each person is tempted when he is coaxed to sin by his own wishes.'"

"But how can we keep from hurting ourselves like those foolish moths when we're tempted?" asked Tom.

"Well," said the man, "that's a good question. God is willing to help us fight our wrong wishes. He's even willing to give us a new spirit."

"I get it," said Tom. "God helps us get rid of wanting to sin."

"Now you see a light that won't hurt you," said the man. "But don't forget that God comes and lives in us through Jesus Christ. Jesus makes us want what God wants, because Jesus is God."

"I know," said Tom. "That's why I'm glad I'm a Christian."

Let's talk about this: What happened to some moths who wanted to get into a street light? Why didn't the moths quit flying at the light? What did the man who cleaned the lamps say to Tom? Why can't we blame God when we hurt ourselves by sinning? How can we keep from following our bad wishes? When does God come into a person's heart and save Him from being tempted?

Bible reading: James 1:13-17.

Let us pray: Dear God and Father in heaven, please forgive us and help us when our own bad wishes lead us into sin. Give us the Holy Spirit so that we will not want to follow our wrong wishes, but will do that which is good. This we ask for the sake of Jesus, our Lord and Savior. Amen.

You will be judged
  by your words. Matthew 12:37

We Are What We Say

Alice found out she could scare people. When she got real angry and said nasty words, the boys and girls would quit teasing her. So she learned to say mean, nasty things. And the more she said them, the meaner she became. She even thought she had a right to be hateful.

Her mother was a kind, Christian woman. She knew Alice needed help, and she wanted to help her daughter become sweeter. One day she told Alice what Jesus once said about the words we speak.

Jesus told His enemies: "How can bad people like you say good things? The words of your mouth come from what's in your heart. The good man gives good things out of his good heart, and the evil man gives evil things out of his evil heart. In the day when God will judge people, you will be judged by your words."

Our words tell what kind of person we really are. Sometimes we can say nice things and not mean them, or we can say bad things and be sorry for them. But, as Jesus said,

140

before we know it, our words give us away. They are like the fruit on a tree. They show what kind of tree we are.

"You see," Alice's mother said to her, "we don't only *talk* the way we *are*, but we also *are* the way we *talk*. Since we belong to Jesus and are God's children, we want to be God's children more and more also in the way we talk."

Alice agreed, and guess what: As Alice thought more about Jesus, she talked more about Him. And when she tried to please Him in what she said, she said mostly kind and good words and hardly ever said mean and unhappy words any more.

Let's talk about this: How do you think Alice felt in her heart when she said mean things? What did Jesus tell His enemies about their words? What do you think they said about Him? What do people say about Jesus when they believe in Him? How does Jesus change people's ways of talking? What did Jesus mean when He said, "You will be judged by your words"?

Bible reading: Matthew 12:33-37.

Let us pray: Dear Father in heaven, like Alice we often say evil words because we are sinners, but we are sorry. Please forgive us for Jesus' sake, and help us to show by all our words that we love You. Amen.

*In quietness and in trust you will
be strong.* Isaiah 30:15

Like Learning to Swim

"In a way learning to swim is like becoming a Christian, isn't it?" said a boy to his swimming teacher.

"How do you mean that?" asked the teacher.

"Well," said the boy, "you told us to throw ourselves into the water and not be afraid of it. You said it would hold us up if we wouldn't fight it."

"Yes, but how is this like becoming a Christian?" asked the teacher.

"Well," said the boy, "to be a Christian, don't you have to trust God to hold you up? My pastor said you have to throw yourself into the arms of Jesus."

The boy was right. To become a Christian we have to trust that Jesus is our Savior. To be a Christian we have to throw ourselves on God's love and trust that He will help us. It's like a swimmer who trusts the water or a little child who trusts that his father will catch him and hold him.

The boy who is afraid of water will never be a good swimmer. The person who doesn't trust God's love will never be a strong and happy child of God. But the person who calmly and cheerfully trusts God will be a strong Christian.

In the Book of Isaiah God says, "In quietness and in trust you will be strong." That means we become strong Christians when we quietly believe the promises of God. He has promised to love us through Jesus, our Savior. Quietly believe that, and you will be strong.

Some questions: What did the little boy tell his swimming teacher? In what way is becoming a Christian like learning to swim? What must a person believe in order to be a Christian? What did God say will make us strong Christians? How does trusting in God's love help us to be strong and happy Christians?

Bible reading: Psalm 71:1-5.

Let us pray: Lord God, our Father in heaven, thank You for promising to give us Your love through our Savior Jesus. Give us the Holy Spirit so that we will quietly trust in Your love. Please make us strong and happy Christians through a quiet trust in Jesus. Amen.

You have been set free from sin
and have become slaves of God. Romans 6:22

Who Will Get You?

Johnny's father wasn't a good man. He often stayed away from home and drank whiskey all night long or came home drunk. Instead of teaching his boy to love God, Johnny's father used God's name for saying mean things.

Johnny's mother tried to teach him and take care of him by herself as well as she could. One day when Billy asked her if Johnny could go along with him to Sunday school, he said, "I wish he would."

A few Sundays later Johnny was in Sunday school ahead of time, and so was his teacher, Mr. Ritter.

"Johnny," said Mr. Ritter, "what do you think you'll be when you grow up?"

"That depends on who gets me," said Johnny.

Mr. Ritter was rather puzzled. "What do you mean?" he asked.

"Well, if the devil gets me, I may be a drunk, like my father. If God gets me, maybe I'll be a minister," Johnny explained.

"You're a wise young man," said Mr. Ritter. "Let's hope that God will get you and will also keep you. He'll be glad to have you be one of His children."

The Bible says we belong to whomever we obey. When we sin, then we are slaves of sin, and the devil has us in his power. When we obey God, then we are His servants and try to please Him.

That's why the apostle Paul said to Christians, "Thanks be to God. You were once slaves of sin, but now you have become slaves of righteousness," which means goodness. "You have been set free from sin and have become slaves of God."

How does this happen? It happens when people believe that Jesus died for their sins and when they begin to live with Him in their hearts. Jesus sets people free from sin and makes them servants of God. That's why it's so important to belong to Him.

Let's talk this over: What did Mr. Ritter ask Johnny? What did Johnny say? What did Johnny think he might be someday if God would get him? Who has us in his power when we sin? Who sets people free from sin? How will we show that we really belong to God?

Bible reading for older children and grownups: Romans 6:16-23.

Let us pray: Lord Jesus, we thank You for setting us free from sin. We are glad that we belong to God. Please help us to learn what You want us to do, and make us willing and able to do it for Your sake. Amen.

Come near to God, and He will come near to you. James 4:8

How Far Away Is God?

"Daddy," said little Mary, "is God 'way up there where the airplane is?"

"Sure, honey," he said.

"And when it flies far away, is God where the airplane is then?"

"Yes, God is there, too," he answered.

"Is God always far away?" asked the little girl.

"No," said her father. "God is everywhere, and He's also very close to us."

"How can I be real close to God?" asked the little girl.

"Well," said her father, "there's a Bible verse that tells you. It says, 'Come near to God, and He will come near to you.'"

"But how can I come near to God?" she asked.

145

"That's not hard," said her father. "All you have to do is listen to what He has said in the Bible and think about what He has done for you and what He wants you to do. You can also come near to Him by talking to Him in prayer."

"You mean, all I have to do is think about God and talk to Him?" asked Mary.

"Yes," said her father, "and believe that He loves you and that He sent Jesus to save you. When you believe that, then God is very close to you."

"I can easily believe that," said Mary, " 'cause I already know that Jesus died for me. He wouldn't have done that if He didn't love me." And she was right.

Something to think about: What did the little girl ask her daddy? What did he tell her? Where else is God? What Bible verse did the father teach his girl? How can we come near to God? Why was the little girl sure that God loved her?

Bible reading: Genesis 28:10-16.

Let us pray: Heavenly Father, thank You for coming near to us when we come to you, asking You to love us for Jesus' sake. Help us to come near to You every day so that You will always be near to us, through Jesus Christ, our Lord. Amen.

As the heaven is high above the earth,
so great is God's mercy. Psalm 103:11

No End to God's Love

"I wish I could jump as high as a telephone pole," said Jack.

"I wish I could jump as high as our hotel," said Ken.

"I wish I could jump as high as the Empire State Building," said Jack. "That's the highest in the world."

"I wish I could jump as high as the sky," said Ken.

"There's nothing that high," said Jack.

"Oh, yes, there is," said Jack's dad, who happened to be listening. "If you'll look up Psalm 103, verse 11, you'll find something that's as high as the sky above the earth."

Jack and Kenny both ran to get their Bibles. Jack had a King James Bible. Ken had a newer translation. When they found the verse, Jack read it: " 'As the heaven is high above the earth, so great is His mercy toward them that fear Him.' What is mercy?" asked Jack.

"My Bible says 'love,'" answered Ken.

"But you can't pile up love like a mountain, can you?" said Jack.

"God wants to tell us there is no end to His love, Jack," said his father. "Mercy is His forgiving love. It goes on and on for those who believe Him and trust that Jesus is their Savior. That's why the Bible says, 'As the heaven is high above the earth, so great is God's mercy.'"

Questions to talk about: What were Jack and Ken wishing? What did Jack's dad ask the boys to do? What did the psalm verse say? What is another word for mercy? Why does God want us to know how great His love is?

Bible reading: Psalm 103:8-12.

Let us bow in prayer: Dear Father in heaven, how terrible it would be if Your love would ever end! Because we sin so much, we need so much love. We are glad that Your love is higher than the sky and deeper than the ocean. Please keep us happy in Your great love for the sake of Jesus, our Savior. Amen.

Everyone who is proud is disgusting to the Lord. Proverbs 16:5

Pete's Trouble

"I'm the best player on the baseball team. Out of the way, Shrimp; let a *man* go by," said Pete as he pushed Joe out of his way.

It was hard to like Pete. He always acted so rough and proud as if he owned the team and the field and the school and everything else in the world.

"Did I tell you how I hit two homers in one game?" he would say with a loud voice when he came up to a group of boys and girls. Even if they were talking about something else, he'd start bragging about himself.

When Pete noticed that he didn't have any friends, he tried to blame others. He said, "They're all jealous. They know I'm the best player and the best wrestler and an all-around champion. That's why all these little punks hate me. Jealous, that's what they are."

By and by most of the children were disgusted with Pete. The worst was that God also gets disgusted with people who are proud and think they are IT. The Bible says, "Everyone who is proud is disgusting to the Lord."

This is true especially when a person acts proud in front of God. We often sin, and we make many mistakes. We're never as good as God wants us to be.

So it's foolish to think we are good. It's much better to bow our heads and say, "Dear God, please forgive us our sins for Jesus' sake and help us do better." When we say this and mean it, we get forgiveness and many other blessings from God. We also become more lovable.

But the proud person is disgusting to the Lord as well as to people. So let's not spoil our life with God by being proud.

Let's talk about this: Why did Pete lose all his friends? What made Pete brag the way he did? How does God feel about proud people? Why is it foolish to think we are good? What is the way to get forgiveness from God? How can we show people that we aren't proud?

A Bible story about two men, one who was proud and one who was not: Luke 18:9-14.

Let us pray: Dear Father in heaven, please forgive all the proud thoughts we have ever had about ourselves. Love us for Jesus' sake, and give us the Holy Spirit so that we will admit our faults and will depend on You for our goodness. In Jesus' name we ask it. Amen.

149

How can a young man keep his way clean?
By guarding it with God's Word. Psalm 119:9

When to Cut Thistles

On the Miller farm there was a big patch of thistles near the house. Thistles are weeds that have sharp points on them. One day Ray said to his father, "Today I'm going to cut down those thistles in our yard."

"That's fine, Ray," said his father. "You promised to do it long ago. I'm glad you're finally going to do it now."

So Ray cut down the thistles, but he got so many scratches from them that his arms started to bleed. Ray's mother had to put bandages on his arms.

A few weeks later his father said, "Look, Ray, this is how I would cut those thistles." Then he took a hoe and quickly chopped off the new thistles that were coming out of the ground. "See," said Ray's father, "not even a scratch."

"Sure, but they were a lot smaller than the ones I had to cut," said Ray.

"Well," said his father, "you should have cut the thistles when they were young. And remember, there are other kinds of weeds that can hurt you more than thistles. Your quick

150

temper is a sharp weed, and your mean teasing, and not doing things when you should, and not caring about other people. These are all thistles that can hurt your life. Be sure to cut them before they get big," said his father.

In Psalm 119 the writer asked himself a question. He said, "How can a young man keep his way clean?" How can he keep the thorns and thistles of sin from growing in his life?

Weeds will grow in every garden. No one can keep them out altogether. But we can dig them up or cut them down. And they're easier to get rid of when they're just starting to grow.

In the same way, sins are like weeds in the garden of our heart. When we ask God to take away our sins for Jesus' sake, He plows them up. But even in a plowed field they keep popping up. So we need to cut them as soon as we notice them.

"How can a young man keep his way clean? By guarding it with God's Word," says the Bible. God's Word points out to us the weeds we need to cut before they grow big and hurt us.

Questions to talk about: Why did the thistles hurt Ray? What did Ray's father show him? What usually is the best way to get rid of weeds? How does Jesus take away the weeds of sin in our hearts? How can a young boy or girl keep the thistles of sin from growing big in his life?

Bible reading: Proverbs 3:1-7.

Let us pray: Dear Jesus, please take away all my sins, and give me a new clean heart every day. When the thorns of sins begin to grow in my life, help me to cut them out at once before they grow big and become hard to get rid of. Amen.

I wish I could die and be with Christ. . . .
But to go on living is more necessary. Philippians 1:23, 24

A Good Reason for Living

In the city where this book was printed there was a young man who had a much longer nose than most people. Almost every day somebody in his school teased him about his nose. When he looked at himself in the mirror, he thought no girl would ever like him. So he took a gun and killed himself.

Did he have to do this? Oh, no. God wanted him to go on living. One of God's commandments is, "You are not to kill," and this includes killing yourself.

Many homely boys marry very nice girls. The boy couldn't change his nose, but he could have been so kind and friendly that people would have liked him anyway.

A very famous inventor named Steinmetz was a homely hunchback. But he did many wonderful things, and his name is in our history books. Abraham Lincoln had an ugly face, but think of how people admire him for what he did.

The apostle Paul had a good reason for wanting to die. He said, "I wish I could die and be with Christ." But did he kill himself? Why, he wouldn't think of it. He knew that would be very wrong. He knew God had some work for him to do here on earth. He said, "To go on living is more necessary."

That's what the boy with the long nose should have said. He should have said, "I will use my life for God in helping other people. I will try to help people get to know Jesus and His love. I will live for Jesus as long as He lets me live."

Jesus has good reasons for letting us live. Even though it will be wonderful to be with Him in heaven, it is necessary for us to go on living on earth as long as He wants us to do so.

Let's talk about this: Why did a boy kill himself? Why was it wrong to do so? What could the boy have done? Why did St. Paul want to die? What did he say was more necessary? When are we ready to die? What good reason do we always have for going on living?

Bible reading for older children and adults: Philippians 1:20-26.

Let us pray: Father in heaven, we know that You made us for a good reason, and we pray that You will show us what You want us to do in this world. Please keep us from ever wanting to stop living, and make us willing to serve You until You are ready to take us to heaven. In Jesus' name we pray this. Amen.

You should love your neighbor
as yourself. Leviticus 19:18

How to Love Others

"Somebody ought to tell Mr. White that his boy steals," said Charles.

"Not I," said June. "That's a good way to get into trouble."

So Charles and June didn't tell Mr. White, and his boy kept on stealing. One day the police caught him stealing a car, and he was sent away to jail.

Wouldn't it have been much better if Charles and June had talked to Mr. White, and to the boy, too? Maybe they could have helped before it was too late.

153

Long ago, already in the Old Testament, God said, "You should love your neighbor as yourself." Later, when Jesus was on earth, He said, "The most important commandment is, 'You should love the Lord, your God, with all your heart and with all your soul and with all your mind and with all your strength.' The second is this, 'You should love your neighbor as yourself.' There is no other commandment greater than these."

What does it mean to love your neighbor as yourself? One time Jesus put this law of God in another way. He said, "Whatever you wish that others would do to you, do that to them." This is called the Golden Rule.

Would we want someone to tell us about our boy's stealing if we were Mr. or Mrs. White? Would we want other people to keep us out of trouble or to help us when we are in trouble? Yes, of course we would.

This doesn't mean we should "butt into" other people's business. But when we can keep someone from getting into trouble or when we can help someone, God wants us to do so. "You should love your neighbor as yourself."

And "neighbor" doesn't only mean the people who live next door to us. It means "brother-man." It means anybody. It means people.

Of course, nobody wants to love other people the way he loves himself. That's why Jesus had to save us. But Jesus makes us willing and able to do so. He gives us the Holy Spirit. Let us ask Him for the Holy Spirit.

Questions to talk about: Why didn't June want to tell Mr. White that his boy was stealing? Why should she have done so anyway? How much did God say we should love our neighbor? Who is our neighbor? How important did Jesus say this commandment is? What do we need from God because we so often do not keep this commandment? Who will help us to love others the way we want to be loved?

154

Bible reading: Mark 12:28-34.

Let us pray: Dear Jesus, You loved us more than You loved Yourself. Please help us to learn from You how to love others, and forgive our selfish love. Give us the Holy Spirit so that we will love others the way we would like to be loved. Amen.

There are many ways of working, but it is the same God who makes people willing to do the different kinds of work for Him. 1 Corinthians 12:6

Many Ways of Serving Jesus

Sue and Ann were twins 'way up in the lumber country in Oregon. While they were still in high school, they started a Sunday school all by themselves in one of the little lumber towns.

When they were through high school, they said, "If one of us could be a nurse, she could earn enough money so the other one could work for Jesus every day all day long. The children in these towns need to learn much more about God and His Word."

155

"That's a wonderful idea," said Ann. "I don't even know which I'd rather be. A nurse can work for Jesus, too. Here, I'll break this toothpick. Then I'll hold the two pieces. If you draw the short one, you study to be a nurse. If you draw the long one, then I'll try to become a nurse."

Sue got the short piece. So she went to nurse's training. This may not have been a good way to decide what to do, but the girls didn't care who won. They both just wanted to do something for Jesus.

While Sue studied to be a nurse, Ann got herself a job to help pay for her sister's training. Ann also kept on teaching children on Sunday mornings.

When Sue became a nurse, she earned good pay and gave half of it to her sister. Then Ann quit her job, bought a little car, and started going to fourteen different little towns every week. Each day she visited homes, told Bible stories to children, and helped them learn about Jesus and His love.

The Bible says, "There are many ways of working, but it is the same God who makes people willing to do the different kinds of work for Him." God the Holy Spirit leads us to love Jesus and His work, and those who really love Him want to work for Him.

And those who really want to work for Jesus don't worry much about the way. They gladly do whatever they can for Him because He does so much for them.

Questions to think about: How did the twin girls work for God while they were still in high school? What did they do after they finished high school? How did one help the other do God's work? Which one do you think served God best? What does the Bible verse say? What are some other ways in which people work for Jesus? What might we do for Him?

Bible reading for grownups: 1 Corinthians 12:4-11.

Let us pray: O Holy Spirit, make us willing to live for Jesus, who died for us. Since there are many ways to work for Him, please help us to find the best ways so that His love will come also to others as it has come to us. Amen.

God's Word have I hid in my heart
that I might not sin. Psalm 119:11

How Mike Learned a Bible Verse

"I can't learn this Bible verse," said Mike. Learning was hard for Mike. His sister Mary had no trouble at all, but Mike did.

"Why don't you study the way Mary does?" Mike's grandmother asked him.

"No two people are alike," said his mother. "We love Mary the way she is, and we love Mike the way he is. Book learning is easier for Mary, but being happy and friendly is easier for Mike."

Then Mike tried to learn that verse again. "Which Bible verse is it?" his mother asked.

"This one," said Mike, and read it to her: "God's Word have I hid in my heart that I might not sin."

"Let's see if I can make it easier for you," said Mike's father, who was listening. "This verse tells of a good thing in a good place for a good reason. Which is the good thing and the good place and the good reason?"

Mike read the verse again. "God's Word — is that the good thing?"

"Yes, go on," said his father.

"God's Word have I hid in my heart," he read. "That must be the good place — my heart."

"And what is the good reason for hiding the good thing in the good place?" his father asked.

"'That I might not sin.' That's a good reason," said Mike.

Now Mike knew the three parts: the good thing, in a good place, for a good reason. With that help Mike could easily say the verse from memory. What's more, he also learned what the verse teaches. He learned that God's Word in his heart would keep Him from sinning.

Even when children have trouble memorizing Bible passages, they usually can do so with a little help. And memorizing God's Word hides it deep down in their heart, and that helps to keep them from sinning.

Questions to talk about: What did Mike have a hard time learning? How did Mike's father help him learn his memory verse? What is the good thing to hide? What is the good place to hide it? What is the good reason for hiding the good thing in the good place? Who can say the Bible verse from memory?

Bible reading: Psalm 119:9-16.

Let us pray: Dear Lord, please help us to hide Your Word in our heart. Help us to remember Your love and to know Your will. And give us the Holy Spirit so that we will gladly obey You out of love for Jesus, our Savior. Amen.

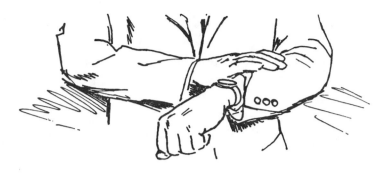

*Jesus said, "If you continue in My Word . . .
you will know the truth.* John 8:31, 32

When a Man's Watch Stopped

"I have plenty of time to catch my train," said Mr. Burr. So he sat down and read the paper. A little later he looked at his watch again. It was still the same time as before.

"Oh, oh," he said, "my watch stopped."

Then he hurried to get to the station. But before he got there, the train pulled out. So he missed the train because his watch had told him the wrong time when it stopped running.

Some people miss life with God and heaven because their religion tells them something wrong. And that's a lot worse than missing a train. How can we know what is the truth about God and heaven? Jesus said, "If you continue in My Word . . . you will know the truth."

We have family devotions because we want to stay with Jesus. We study the Bible in order to keep on believing what He has said. We go to church to hear and learn His Word so that we will know more about the truth.

It is important to continue believing the Bible. The Bible is the Word of God. It tells us what Jesus wants us to believe. And it is the truth. Whoever tells us something dif-

159

ferent is wrong, because Jesus is right. He can't be wrong. He is God.

What does the Bible say about God and the way to heaven? It says, "Believe on the Lord Jesus Christ, and you will be saved." It says we will get to heaven by trusting that Jesus will take us there. It says, "Christ died for all." It says, "The blood of Jesus Christ, God's Son, cleanses us from all sin." When Jesus suffered and died, He paid for our sins. Those who believe this get God's forgiveness.

The Bible also tells us what is right and wrong. It tells how we can please God. And it's all true. If we don't keep on believing what the Bible says, our Christian faith stops. Then, like a watch that has stopped, our religion begins to tell us wrong things.

To keep from missing the train to heaven, let us continue to hear and read and study and believe the teachings of Jesus. Then we will know what is true. We will know the truth.

Let's talk about this: Why did the man miss his train? In what way is a wrong religion like a wrong watch? How can we know what is true about God and life with God? What did Jesus say we must keep on doing in order to know what is true? What will help to keep us with Jesus and His Word? What does the Bible say is the only true way to heaven? Let's say the Bible verse together.

Bible reading: 2 Timothy 3:14-17.

Let us pray: Dear Jesus, please help us to keep on believing Your Word. Bless our reading of the Bible, our family devotions, our church and church schools, and anything else that helps us to know the truth about life with God. Please keep us from ever believing any teachings that are not true, so that we will not miss being with You forever in heaven through Your love. Amen.

Let us not get tired
  of doing good. Galatians 6:9

Never Too Tired to Do Good

The telephone rang in the middle of a cold, rainy night. The pastor answered, half asleep. The voice over the telephone said, "My wife is very sick. The ambulance is taking her to the hospital. I think she's going to die. Please go to see her right away."

The pastor dressed in a hurry, grabbed his coat and hat, and hurried out into the dark night.

By then his little girl Susan was awake, too, and was sitting up in bed.

"Mommy," said little Susan after the minister had gone, "people often call Daddy at night. Daddy needs to sleep. Doesn't he ever get tired of helping people?"

"Honey," said her mother, "your daddy has learned a Bible verse that helps him. Would you like to learn it?"

"Uh-huh," said the girl.

So the mother sat down beside Susan and told her what the Bible tells all of us. "Let us not get tired of doing good."

"Daddy never gets tired of doing good," said Susan.

"Oh, sometimes he does," said her mother, "but your daddy is glad he can do good for people. He loves Jesus, and someday Jesus will say to Him, 'What you did for others you did for Me.'"

"I know," said Susan. "Even if you give just a drink of water to someone because you love Jesus, it's the same as giving it to Jesus. May I have a drink, Mommy?" she asked, grinning with two front teeth missing.

"Sure, but then we'd better go to sleep," said her mother. "Otherwise we might be too tired to do good tomorrow."

Our questions: Why did the pastor's phone ring in the middle of the night? Why did the pastor get dressed and leave? What Bible verse did Susan's mother teach her? What did Jesus say about the good things people do to others?

Bible reading: Matthew 25:31-40.

Let's talk to God about this: Lord God, we are glad that You never get tired of being good to us. Please forgive us when we get tired of doing all the good we can. Keep us from ever getting tired of doing good. In Jesus' name we ask this. Amen.

As many of you as were baptized
into Christ have put on Christ. Galatians 3:27

When Tony Was Adopted

Tony was an adopted boy. After he lived with his new father and mother for a year, they were allowed to sign some papers. The papers said he was really and truly their own son. Now nobody could ever say he didn't belong to them.

Of course, Tony's new parents loved him before they signed the adoption papers, but they loved him even more after he belonged to them for keeps.

Baptism is almost like adoption papers. All who believe in Jesus are adopted children of God. Some people do not learn about Jesus until they are older. Some first believe in Jesus, and then they are baptized. But many start to believe through Baptism.

The Bible says, *"As many of you as were baptized into Christ have put on Christ."* Through Baptism people receive

162

the faith in Jesus which makes them children of God. It is faith in the forgiveness of all sins — the washing away by God of all that is wrong with a person.

Long ago fathers gave special coats to their children to show who belonged to them. In being baptized, Christians receive and put on the coat of Jesus Christ. This means His name and life and everything He wants to give us.

Baptism is God's way of signing our adoption papers. That's why Baptism can be called our second birthday, the day when we are adopted into God's family as a brother or sister of Jesus. And do you know the most wonderful thing about being adopted by God? His children are given a home in heaven!

That's why we must never forget our Baptism. It helps us remember that we have been adopted and that we belong to God.

Let's talk about this: How did Tony get some new parents? Why were the papers important? What happens when people are baptized? What is so wonderful about being adopted by God?

Bible reading: Galatians 3:26-29.

Let us pray. Dear Father in heaven, we thank You for having adopted us into Your family of children who believe in Jesus and His love. Please wash away all our sins every day, and keep us forever as Your children, through Jesus Christ, our Lord. Amen.

A glad heart makes a cheerful face. Proverbs 15:13

How to Be Cheerful

"Nothing ever goes right for me," said Jane. "I wanted to be invited to Susan's party and I wasn't. I wanted to go swimming this afternoon, and now it's raining. I wanted to watch the murder movie on TV, and Mother wouldn't let me. Everything is always wrong for me."

That's the way Jane whined and complained. It wasn't good for her, either. She made herself feel sick and unhappy. She walked around with a long, sad face. She made other people feel bad, too.

The Bible says, "A glad heart makes a cheerful face, but by sadness of heart the spirit is broken." Because Jane was sad, her face was sad, and she didn't have much spirit for anything.

How could Jane live without a sad face and a sick spirit? Well, she could say, "I have lots of reasons for being happy.

164

Jesus loves me, and God is good to me. I have a nice home and good parents. I'll do something for Mother or invite a friend to come over. Being happy is more important than seeing a movie or going to a party."

Jane could have enjoyed helping someone — perhaps a sister or a neighbor. She could have tried to make someone else happy. Then she would have felt better and she would have looked better.

When we believe in Jesus, then Jesus lives in us and gives us the Holy Spirit. The Holy Spirit gives us a glad heart and a cheerful face because with Jesus we know that everything turns out good for us. That's another reason for keeping Jesus in our hearts. Jesus can keep us happy, no matter what happens.

Questions to think about: Why was Jane sad? How did her sad heart make her look? How do you think she acted? What does the Bible verse say? Why does knowing Jesus give us a glad heart? What kind of face does Jesus want us to have, a sour face or a cheerful face? Let's try smiling more tomorrow.

Bible reading: Psalm 100.

Our prayer: Dear God, help us always to remember how much You love us so that we won't fret and complain when our own little plans and wishes go wrong. Please give us the Holy Spirit all the time, and make us happy and cheerful Christians, through Jesus Christ, our Savior. Amen.

Turn away from evil. Proverbs 3:7

A Good Rule for Your Club

Six boys were starting a club. They were talking about rules for their club.

"Let's have a rule that every member must skip school once a month," said Tom. "That'll keep out the sissies."

"Yeah, and let's make every member try to get past the bus driver without paying. That'll be fun," said Dick.

"Well, I guess I can't join your club," said Bob. "If you don't want to do things God's way, I don't want to belong."

"Aw, these rules are just to show we're not sissies," said Dick.

"I'd rather follow a Bible rule which says, 'Turn away from evil.' And you should, too," Bob told them. "You're all Christians, aren't you?"

"Sure, but where'd you find that rule?" asked Tom.

"In the Bible. I'll show you the next time, if you want to see it," said Bob. "It could be the first rule of our club, and then we'd have something we wouldn't have to be ashamed of."

Windy hadn't said anything so far. He had been worrying about doing wrong. But now he jumped up. "That's the ticket," he said. "I'd like that for our first rule."

So they agreed that the first rule of the club should be, "Turn away from evil." And wasn't that a much better rule for a group of young Christians than the ones Tom and Dick had suggested?

It's a good rule for any club. You see, Jesus came and died to save us from sin. He wants to belong to our club, too. If we want Jesus in our club, we can't plan to do anything wrong. He won't belong if we do.

166

Let's think about this: Which rules did Tom and Dick want for their club? What did Bob say about this? Which rule did Bob want? Why was this a much better rule? How can we have Jesus in our club? Why won't He belong to a club that plans anything wrong?

Bible reading: Proverbs 1:10-15.

Let us bow in prayer: We thank You, dear Father in heaven, for friends who help us turn away from evil. Please give us many such friends, and make us glad always to do things Your way. We ask this in the name of Jesus, who saved us so that we would live holy lives for Him. Amen.

You, God, see me. Genesis 16:13

When God Sees Us

"I don't like God," said Ned. He was only four years old and didn't understand God very well.

"Why don't you like God, honey?" his mother asked. She knew that Ned needed to understand God better.

"'Cause God always watches me when I do bad," said Ned.

"Don't you like me and Daddy?" his mother asked.

"Sure," said Ned.

167

"Well, *we* watch you when you do bad things," his mother told him.

"But you help me when I'm bad," he said.

"Honey, God does, too," she said. "Yesterday you ran across the street, even though you shouldn't. God saw you and kept the cars from hitting you. He was good to you. But I think He's waiting for you to tell Him you're sorry."

"I'm sorry, Mommie," said Ned. "When I'm sorry, does God forgive me?"

"Yes," said his mother, "He forgives you because He loves you. And do you remember why He can forgive you?"

" 'Cause Jesus paid for my bad," said Ned. And then his mother knew that Ned loved God again, and Ned was ready for his prayers and bed.

The Bible tells us that God sees all that we do. But when God watches us, He does it with love. And when we do wrong, He teaches us that it is wrong and hopes we'll come and ask Him for forgiveness. For Jesus' sake He's always willing to forgive us, and this makes us want to be better.

Some important questions: Why didn't Ned like God? Why don't we want anyone to see what we do wrong? Why is it good that God always sees what we do? When we do wrong, for what does God wait? Why is God always willing to forgive us when we are sorry about our sins?

Bible reading about someone God watched: Genesis 16:6-14.

Let us pray: Dear Father in heaven, we are glad that You never sleep and that You are always watching over us. Please watch that nothing really bad happens to us. When we do wrong, please forgive us and help us to change. When we do right, help us to feel happy about it. In Jesus' name we ask it. Amen.

A tattler tells secrets, but a person who has a right spirit keeps them hidden. Proverbs 11:13

Is Tattling Wrong?

The Meyers were eating supper, and Freddy Meyer was thinking about what had happened at school that day.

"Joe always tells the teacher everything we do," said Fred. "It's wrong to be a tattletale, isn't it, Dad?"

"That depends on what a person tells," said his dad. "Maybe Joe wants the teacher to help the children behave better."

"No, he just likes to tattle," said Fred; "and it's never anything very important."

"Joe is a mean boy," said his sister Virginia. "He's a regular old gossip. He's always talking about other people."

"Well, isn't somebody talking about somebody at our supper table tonight?" her mother asked.

Virginia looked at Fred and giggled. All at once she realized they had been tattling about Joe.

Sometimes things should be told. When our telling is helpful and will keep a person from doing wrong, then we must tell what we know. But most tattling is wrong because it is gossip. Gossip hurts people and helps nobody.

The Bible says, "A tattler tells secrets, but a person who has a right spirit keeps them hidden." This is true of secrets people tell us. It is also true of bad things we find out about people. These we ought not tell because they won't help anyone.

Jesus died for our sins. He wants to save us also from a tattling tongue. When we love Him and people, we don't tell things that should be kept a secret.

169

Questions to talk about: When is it right to tell a secret we know? When is it wrong? Why was Joe's tattling wrong? What does the Bible verse say about a tattletale or tattler? What kind of person tries to keep a secret? How does our love of Jesus keep us from having a tattling tongue?

Bible reading: Proverbs 11:9-13.

Let us pray: Father in heaven, we have enough to do to keep track of our own badness. Please keep us from talking about other people. Help us to say what is good and what is helpful. Make us willing to keep bad things a secret unless we can help someone by telling on them. We ask this in Jesus' name. Amen.

She has done what she could. Mark 14:8

A Little Light That Saved a Life

A long time ago a young boy was traveling across the ocean on a sailing ship. Just before he went to bed one night, he heard someone shouting, "Man overboard!" Then he heard the feet of many people running on the deck above him.

"What can I do?" he asked himself. "Up there I'll only be in the way."

Then an idea came to him. He took the light that was hanging from the ceiling of his cabin and held it out of

170

the porthole, the ship's window. He did this so that the light would shine on the water.

By and by he heard a voice yell, "We have him," and then some people in the crowd above shouted, "He's saved!"

The next day the captain told the people on the ship that the boy's light from the porthole helped them save the man who was drowning. The boy had done what he could, and it helped very much.

We usually are most helpful when we do what we can where we are. And Christians have a special reason for doing what they can. They have the love of Jesus in their hearts.

Once a woman named Mary wanted to do something to show that she loved Jesus. So she came and poured some very expensive perfume on His head and feet. When some people scolded her for doing this, Jesus said, "Let her alone. . . . She has done a good work. . . . She has done what she could."

In another place the Bible says, "Whatever your hand finds to do, do it with your might." God wants us to do whatever we can as well as we can. The love of Jesus makes us want to do our very best for Him. Nothing but our best is good enough when we are giving Jesus our life.

Let's talk about this: What happened on the ship? What did the boy do to help? Why was this the best he could have done? What special reason do we have for doing what we can to help people? How are we to do whatever we do?

Bible reading about some people who helped the apostle Paul: Romans 16:1-6.

We bow to pray: Dear Lord, please lead us to do whatever we can for You and for people. Help us to do it with all our might for the sake of Jesus, our Savior, who did so much for us. Amen.

Who can say, "I have made my heart clean"? Proverbs 20:9

Our Clean Isn't Clean

"Larry, did you wash? Are your hands and face clean?" his mother asked when he came to the table.

"Sure," he said. "I'm clean. I washed myself good."

But when Larry's mother looked at him closely, she saw that his ears were dirty, his face wasn't washed under his chin, and his hands had dirt between the fingers.

"Do you call that clean?" Larry's mother asked him as she showed him his hands.

"It looks clean to me," he said.

"Your clean isn't clean," she told him and made him go back and wash again. When he came back and still wasn't clean, she marched back to the washroom with him and finished the job herself.

Many people talk as Larry did when God tells them their heart must be clean for them to live with Him in heaven. They say, "We're clean. We washed ourselves. We did some good things." But when God looks them over, He sees that their hearts are full of sin. Their clean isn't clean.

In our Bible verse God asks, "Who can say, I have made my heart clean"? The answer is "Nobody." Nobody can make himself real clean from sin. We all need to ask God to wash away the dirt of sin.

When Larry's mother washed him, he was really clean. When God wipes away all our sins by forgiving us for Jesus' sake, then we are clean from top to toe. Then we are really clean.

Questions to talk about: Who thought Larry was clean? Who didn't think so? How did Larry become clean? What does God say to anybody who thinks he has made himself clean? Which is the only way to get really clean of all sin?

Bible reading for older children and grownups: Romans 4:5-8.

Let us pray: Dear Father in heaven, don't let us ever think we are clean when we really aren't. We want to be with You in heaven, and we know that no one can make himself clean enough for that. So please wash our hearts by forgiving all our sins for Jesus' sake. In His name we ask this. Amen.

I am holy. Psalm 86:2

A Holy Man in a Hardware Store

"Here comes a holy man," said Mr. James to his wife in the hardware store. He didn't want Mr. Brown to hear what he said, but Mr. Brown heard it.

"That's true," said Mr. Brown, "you now have a holy man in your store."

"Ha, ha, ha," laughed Mrs. James from behind the counter.

173

"Go ahead and laugh," said Mr. Brown. "But really the Bible says I'm a holy man."

"Look," said Mr. James, "last time you were in here you tried to tell me all people are sinners. When I said that most people are good, you said, 'Not good enough for God.' Remember? And now you say you're holy."

"But I am," said Mr. Brown.

"Well, you'll have to explain that," said Mr. James.

"All right, I will," said Mr. Brown. "You see, I do many wrong things, so I'm a sinner. But God forgives me for Jesus' sake, because the blood of Jesus Christ, God's Son, cleanses me from all sin, just as the Bible says. So I am also clean and holy. In God's eyes I'm a saint as well as a sinner because He covers up and takes away my sins."

"I see," said Mr. James, who was very serious by now.

"But I'm a holy man in another way," said Mr. Brown. "Because I love Jesus as my Savior, I also want to live my life for Him. In the Bible any person or thing used by God, or chosen to be used for God, was called holy. I'm holy because God wants to use me and because I want to be used by God."

"I thought only saints were holy," said Mrs. James.

"Sure," said Mr. Brown. "But I'm a saint, even though it may not sound right for me to say it. You can be, too. The Bible calls all the followers of Jesus 'saints.' God doesn't call people saints because they are perfect in what they do. They are called saints because they believe in Jesus and have their sins washed away."

That night Mr. and Mrs. James talked for quite a while about Mr. Brown and what he had said.

"So that's why Christians say, 'I believe in . . . the communion of saints,' said Mrs. James. "I'm beginning to think we need the love of Jesus, too."

Let's talk about this: What did Mr. James call Mr. Brown? Why did Mrs. James laugh when Mr. Brown said he was holy? Why would it be right to say that no one but God is holy? In what ways can people be holy? Why does the Bible call all Christians "saints"? Do you think we are holy saints? Do we always act like saints? Why not? How can we change that?

Bible reading: Psalm 86:1-5.

Our prayer: Dear Father in heaven, we are glad that through Your forgiveness we are holy, even though we are sinners. Please forgive us all our sins every day for Jesus' sake, and make us holy also in our living for You. In Jesus' name we ask this. Amen.

We have a Lawyer. 1 John 2:1

A Helper to Get Us Through

Mary and Mark and their mother were coming to America on a ship. Their father was dead. They were very poor. They had been in a camp for people without homes. Someone in America had promised to take care of them.

"What must we do when we land?" Mark asked the man traveling with them. "We can't talk English very well. We haven't any money. And we don't know how to act in America."

The man smiled and said, "Don't worry. I'll help you. That's why I'm here. I'll see that you get through to where you're going. And at the other end you have a lawyer who will take care of you."

Mark ran to his mother. "The man said he'll help us land and we have a lawyer in America who will take care

175

of us," Mark told his mother and sister. Then they all felt much better. They could hardly wait to get to their new home.

Some Christians worry about what will happen to them when they die, or what will happen between now and the time when they must meet God. They have many sins. They know they can't pay for their sins themselves. They wonder whether they will get through to their home in heaven, or whether God may refuse to keep them.

The Bible says, "We have a Lawyer." This Lawyer and Friend is Jesus Christ. He is with God the Father in heaven and has arranged a place for us in heaven. He has even paid the cost of our home in heaven by living and dying for us. He will meet us at the end of our trip to heaven and will get us through.

In the meantime we also have people who help us on the way. Can you guess who some of them are?

Questions to help us think: Why was the little family worried? What made them feel better? We are all on a trip to a new home in heaven. Why do we need a Lawyer? Who has promised to get us through? Why is He able to do so?

Bible reading: 1 John 1:7—2:2.

Let us pray: Lord Jesus, we are glad that You are our Lawyer in heaven. Please take care of what we owe God, wash away all our sins with Your love, and help us to get through to our heavenly home. Thank You also for the people who help us on our way. Amen.

He who is lazy in his work is a brother
to him who is a great waster. Proverbs 18:9

There's No Fun Like Work

"How much work do you have to do at home?" Slim asked Paul.

"I'm supposed to clear the table before going to school and make my bed and set the supper table and take care of the lawn and my dog. But I know how to get out of work," said Paul, thinking he was smart.

"How?" asked Slim.

"I waste a lot of time getting ready, and when there's no time left, my mom says, 'Hurry on, get out of here, or you'll be late for school!' Then I don't have to do anything."

"But you'll never learn to work that way," said Slim. "My dad says, 'There's no fun like work.' "

"You think work is fun? Crazy, man," said Paul. "I get out of it when I can."

"But what'll you do when you *have* to work?" Slim asked his friend Paul. "You won't *enjoy* working. Remember what Mr. Lacker said? People who amount to something usually like to work. And God wants us to be useful."

Slim was right. The Bible calls the lazy person wicked. It says, "He who is lazy in his work is a brother to him who is a great waster." A lazy person wastes his time, which is as bad as wasting money or food or our chances to learn and to do good.

God wants us to be useful and busy for Him. We can't be if we're lazy. That's why laziness is a sin for which we need the forgiveness of Jesus, our Savior. When we ask Jesus for forgiveness and mean it, He makes us happy to work. There is really no fun like working hard for God.

Let's think about this: How did Paul feel about work? What did his friend Slim tell him? What does the Bible call a lazy person? What does the lazy person waste? How can we get forgiveness and help for the sin of laziness? Let's say the Bible verse together.

Some Bible verses about laziness: Proverbs 24:30-34.

Let us pray: Lord Jesus, when You were a boy, You were helpful to others. When You were a young man, You worked hard as a carpenter. When You were a preacher and teacher, You hardly had time to eat and sleep. Please make us willing to work hard for You so that we will have a useful and happy life. Amen.

The Lord hates . . . a false witness
who whispers lies. Proverbs 6:19

The Sin of Whispering Lies

Mrs. Burns often came over to Mrs. Scott's house. They liked to have a cup of coffee together, and then they'd just sit and talk.

"You know," said Mrs. Burns, "Rita treats her husband like a dog. And she's a very poor housekeeper."

"I know it," said Mrs. Scott. "Why, one time I saw her putting dishes away that were only half clean."

They talked about many people that way, always telling bad things, most of them lies or half lies.

Rita didn't know why some of her friends were staying away from her. She didn't know that Mrs. Burns and Mrs. Scott were telling lies about her.

One day Mrs. Burns went over to Mrs. Lander's house. There she started to say almost in a whisper, "You know,

178

I must tell you, this Rita across the street is having a lot of trouble with her husband."

Mrs. Lander said, "Oh, I think they get along better than most of our neighbors."

"But she's a very poor housekeeper," said Mrs. Burns.

"You must be wrong," said Mrs. Lander. "She kept house for me when I was sick, and she's the cleanest, neatest person you've ever met."

"Well, good-by, it was nice visiting with you," said Mrs. Burns, but she was angry. She didn't like people who wouldn't listen to her lies.

There are many people like Mrs. Burns. In fact, sometimes we all like to repeat bad stories about people. Many children enjoy whispering lies that get other people into trouble.

But telling lies in a whisper or out loud is a great sin. The Bible says, "The Lord hates . . . a false witness who whispers lies." That is why He has given us the commandment, "You shall not bear false witness against your neighbor."

This sin of telling lies is another reason why Jesus had to suffer and die for us. God would have to punish us if Jesus hadn't paid for our sins. Those who love Jesus try not to tell lies to people or whisper lies about them.

Bible reading: Proverbs 6:12-19.

Questions to talk about: What did Mrs. Burns like to say? How did Mrs. Lander make Mrs. Burns angry? How does the Lord feel about a false witness who whispers lies? Which commandment forbids lying? Why do Christians try to keep from lying?

Let us pray: Lord Jesus, You never told lies or repeated bad stories about anyone. Please let Your good life count for us, and teach us to say only what is good and helpful. Amen.

Jesus said: "It is not the will of My Father who is in heaven that one of these little ones should die." Matthew 18:14

Some Very Foolish Sheep

Billy was helping his father bring home some sheep. There were wolves in the woods nearby. So Billy and his father put the sheep into a safe pen at night.

When Billy opened the little gate in the fence, many of the sheep didn't want to go into the safe place. Some always ran past the gate.

"Let's let them stay out," said Billy. "I'm getting tired. It'll be their own fault if the wolves get them."

"No," said Billy's father, "I don't want any of my sheep to be killed by a wolf." So they kept on trying to get them through the gate.

Jesus once said: "I am the Door of the sheep yard." He is the Door to heaven, the Door through which people must go to be saved and safe. The devil and his angels are like wolves. They want to eat up the sheep and keep them from getting into heaven.

Many people don't know this. They don't want to go through the little Door. They refuse to believe that Jesus is their Savior.

180

Sometimes God's helpers get tired of trying to get the lambs and sheep to go through the little Door. They feel like letting the devil get the people who don't want Jesus to save them.

But Jesus loves us. He said: "My Father in heaven doesn't want a single little lamb to die." Jesus, the Good Shepherd, even died for His Father's sheep. That's why we also should keep on trying to get His lambs and sheep into His church. God wants us to lead children and grownups to believe in Jesus even when they don't want to.

Questions to talk about: Why did Billy and his father try to put their sheep into a safe place? Why was it hard to do this? Why didn't they give up? What did Jesus do to save us? In what way is Jesus the Door of God's sheep yard? What did Jesus say His Father doesn't want? How can we help save people?

Bible reading: Psalm 23. Can you say it by heart?

Let us pray: Dear Father in heaven, thank You for saving us from the devil by bringing us into Your kingdom through Jesus, the Door. Make us willing to help save others, for Jesus' sake. Amen.

*Take your share of hard things as a good soldier
of Jesus Christ.* 2 Timothy 2:3

Following Jesus the Hard Way

"I want to be a doctor," said Warren, "but I don't want to go to college a long time."

"That's the only way to become a doctor," said his brother Bob.

"Then I'll be a lawyer," said Warren.

"You'll have to study law then," said Bob. "That takes quite a few years, too."

"Well, then I'll be a teacher," said Warren.

"Don't you think teachers have to go to school many years?" asked Bob.

"How about a pastor? How long do they have to study?" asked Warren.

"As much as a doctor, and sometimes more," said Bob, grinning. He was planning to be a pastor or a teacher.

"There ought to be an easy way to become a doctor or a lawyer or a teacher or a pastor," Warren grumbled.

"Well, there just isn't," said Bob. "You won't amount to much by just doing the things that are easy. You must be willing to go the hard way."

"But it's easy to be a Christian," said Warren. "All you have to do is believe in Jesus."

"Maybe we could say that *to become* a Christian is easy, but to be a *good* Christian and a *helpful* Christian takes a lot of studying and praying," said his dad. "That's why Paul told Timothy, 'Take your share of hard things as a good soldier of Jesus Christ.'"

Warren thought about this awhile. Then he said, "Maybe

182

I'll become a missionary doctor, even if I have to study a long time. A missionary doctor could help Jesus a lot, couldn't he?"

"Oh, yes," his father agreed. "I'm sure he could."

Let's talk about this: In what way did Warren want to become a doctor or a pastor? What did his brother Bob tell him? What did Paul tell Timothy about being a soldier of Jesus Christ? What do you think he meant? Why is it easy to *become* a Christian? Why is it hard to *be* a good and useful Christian? Why would anyone want to do hard things for Jesus?

Bible reading about Paul's hard life for Jesus: 2 Corinthians 11:23-28.

Our Prayer: Dear Jesus, You didn't follow an easy road when You lived and died to save us and to give us life with God in heaven. Please make us willing to gladly do hard things for You, especially those things that will be helpful to others. Amen.

They desire a better country, that is, a heavenly one. Therefore God is not ashamed to be called their God. Hebrews 11:16

God and All Kinds of People

"Mother, I'm supposed to march in the school parade with Betty," said Jane. You could tell by the face she made that she didn't want to do it.

"What's so bad about that?" her mother asked.

"Betty is never dressed very well," said Jane. "Her parents are poor."

"Is that a reason to be ashamed of her?" asked her mother.

"But Betty isn't like the rest of us," said Jane. "I'll feel silly walking with her."

"Listen, Jane," said her mother. "Betty goes to church with us. She loves the Lord Jesus and will be in heaven with us. I'm sure God isn't ashamed of her."

"How do you know?" asked Jane. She knew the answer, but she was being stubborn.

Jane's mother went and got her Bible. She always took time out for Bible reading even on a busy day, so now she could find the verse she needed. It was marked with a red pencil.

"Look here," she said. "The Book of Hebrews tells about all kinds of people who loved God because they believed His promise of a home with Him in heaven. Hebrews 11:16 says, 'God is not ashamed to be called their God.' God is not ashamed to be called the God of anybody who wants to live with Him and believes His promises. God is not ashamed to be Betty's God."

"But do I have to be friends with everybody?" Jane argued.

Her mother was sad and ashamed that her daughter didn't want to be friendly with all children. She said, "Some people are proud. They think they are too good to be near a person who is poor or from a different country. Others aren't kind and decent to people whose skin is a different color than theirs. But the Bible says, 'In every nation anyone who loves God and does what is right is accepted by God.' If God is not ashamed to be their God, how can we be ashamed to be their friends?"

Jane said no more. But she was friendly with Betty when they marched together in the parade. Later she said to her mother, "I'm glad that God loves all people, especially those who want to be with Him in heaven."

Questions to talk about: What was Jane worrying about? What did her mother tell her? What does God say about anyone who believes His Word? Why are some people ashamed to be friendly with others? Why did Jane try to be friendly with Betty in the parade?

Bible reading: Hebrews 11:13-16.

Let us bow and pray: Lord God, our Father in heaven, we're glad that You are not ashamed of anyone who loves You, and that You are not ashamed of us. Please help us not to be ashamed of being kind and friendly to other people, especially to fellow Christians who are Your children. We ask this in the name of Jesus, who died for all. Amen.

Christ left you an example that you should follow in His steps. 1 Peter 2:21

Following the Pattern

"What's the matter with this old cloth, Mother?" said Judy. She was almost crying. She was learning to sew, but the dress she was making didn't fit and look right.

Judy's mother looked at the dress. "Nothing is wrong with the cloth, honey," she said. "You just didn't follow the pattern."

If Judy had followed the pattern carefully, her dress

185

would have come out all right. A good pattern shows you how to make something real well.

Bigger people than Judy make the same mistake she made.

"What's the matter with our home?" asked Mr. Black. "There's so much quarreling and unhappiness in it."

Shall we tell him what's causing the trouble? He and his family aren't following God's pattern in their home.

"I don't know what's wrong with my life," said Miss George. "I don't even have a good reason for living. I wish I were dead."

Shall we tell Miss George a secret? If she will change her life and will follow the pattern of our Lord Jesus, she will have good reasons for living.

"Our church is a mess," says Mrs. Moss. "In every meeting we quarrel, and no one wants to do any work."

Shall we tell Mrs. Moss the secret of a happy, busy church? The members ought to follow the pattern of our Lord Jesus, who was happy doing His heavenly Father's business already when He was a boy.

The Bible says, "Christ left you an example that you should follow in His steps." Jesus is the Pattern. When we follow Him, our church and our home and our life become much better, much more the way God wants them to be.

Of course, we won't follow Him unless we love Him. That's why He died for us and forgives us our sins — to get us to love Him and to follow Him!

Questions to talk about: Why didn't the dress Judy was making turn out right? What pattern has God given us to follow in our living? What are some of the examples of Jesus we ought to follow? Why will following Jesus give us a good life? What did Jesus do to get us to follow Him?

Bible reading: 1 Peter 2:20-25.

Our prayer: Lord Jesus, we can't love as You loved, nor live as good a life as You lived. Please forgive us. For Your name's sake help us to follow Your pattern closely so that we will be more like You in all that we do. Amen.

God can do much more than all that we ask or think. Ephesians 3:20

They Got More than They Asked For

"I wish Mr. Glass would tell us we could pick some of his cherries. His trees are loaded," said Tom.

"Why don't we ask him?" said Toby, his brother.

"Oh, he'll just say 'No' and try to scare us away," said Tom.

But Toby kept thinking it wouldn't hurt to ask.

One day Toby saw Mr. Glass in his orchard, so he walked over to him and said, "Mr. Glass, do you ever let children pick some of your cherries?"

"I might," said Mr. Glass, "if you'll pick around the bottom and will stay out of the trees. I don't want you to get hurt, you know."

"Oh, boy!" said Toby. "Thanks."

"And when the plums and apples get ripe, you may do

the same," said Mr. Glass. "God gives me much more than I can use for myself."

Toby ran to tell Tom all about it. "We got more than I asked for," he said.

In a way, God is like Mr. Glass. God is glad when we ask Him for things that are good for us, and He gives us much more than we ask. The Bible says, "God can do much more than all that we ask or think." He can even give us everlasting life with Him. He promises to do so through Jesus Christ, our Lord, and He will.

Questions to talk about: What did the boys wish? Why didn't Tom ask Mr. Glass? What did Mr. Glass say when Toby talked to him? In what way is God like Mr. Glass? What is the best gift God wants to give all of us? How can anyone get this gift?

Bible reading: Ephesians 3:14-21.

Our prayer: Dear Father in heaven, help us to believe that You love us and that You will give us much more than all that we ask or think. We are glad that we are Your children through Jesus Christ, Your Son, our Savior. Amen.

The church that is in their house. Romans 16:5

The Family Altar

The first day Judy joined a Sunday school class at Trinity Church, the leader asked them all to bring some money for an altar.

"Why do you need money to have an altar?" asked Judy. She was thinking of the kind of altar that doesn't cost any money.

"Well, we would like to have our own little altar around

which to visit with God, and we can't have an altar unless we can pay someone to make it for us," said the leader.

"In our home we have a family altar, but it's not a table," said Judy.

The leader smiled. "Tell us about it," she said.

So Judy came forward and said, "The first thing my daddy wanted in our new house was family devotions. So when we moved in, we all sat down in the living room, and he read from the Bible. Then we all kneeled and asked God to bless us in our new home. Daddy said our devotions together every day would be our family altar."

"Thank you for telling us about your family altar," said the leader. "I wish all the children had a family altar in their home. When you read and listen to God's Word and pray with your family in your home, then you have family devotions. This is a family altar and church service in your house. It doesn't cost any money."

"Then why do we need money for an altar in Sunday school?" asked Judy.

"Because a special table where we meet with God helps us to think about God. That's why we also want it to be beautiful," the leader explained, "and that's why we put a cross and candles on the altar. They help us to remember that Jesus died for us and is our Savior," said the leader.

Questions to talk about: What did the leader ask Judy's Sunday school class to do? Why was Judy puzzled? What kind of altar did Judy have in her home? What is a family altar? How can an altar of wood help us? Which of the two kinds of altars is most important?

Bible reading about a family altar: Colossians 3:15-17.

Let us bow and pray: Dear God, we are glad that we can pray to You in any place. Bless our family altar by speaking to us and listening to our prayers, and come into our hearts every day, through Jesus Christ, our Lord. Amen.

189

*God dresses the flowers
of the field.* Matthew 6:30

What Flowers Tell About God

"The flowers are beautiful," said little Joan to the lady from the church. The lady had come to see Joan at the hospital. Visiting the sick was one of the ways she worked for God. She had brought the flowers from the church.

"Flowers say many things to us," said the visiting lady. "They talk to us about God."

"They do?" said Joan. She hadn't ever thought about that.

"Yes, they do. They tell us that God loves us," said the lady. "God could have made all the flowers black. But why did He make flowers pretty? Because He knew we would like pretty things."

"Now I can hear the flowers talk," said Joan with a smile. "Here's one with three colors in one blossom, and so soft and lovely."

"Jesus said the flowers tell us not to worry," said the lady. "The flowers never worry about what to wear, but God makes them very pretty anyway. Jesus said the only thing we need to worry about is being a child of God and living in His kingdom."

190

"I'm glad *I'm* a child of God," said Joan. "I believe that Jesus is God and that He died for me."

"Good," said the lady visitor, "then I won't have to worry about you. You have God's forgiveness and His love, and your life is going to be as pretty as a flower." With that she patted Joan's cheeks and left her happier than when she came.

Some questions: What did a lady church visitor say to Joan about flowers? What did Jesus say about flowers? What do flowers say to you? What made Joan happy? Why didn't the visitor worry about Joan?

Bible reading: Matthew 6:28-33.

Let us pray: Dear God, we thank You for the flowers which tell us that You love us. We thank You most of all for the love of Jesus, who suffered and died so that we could be Your children. Please live in our hearts and make our lives as beautiful as flowers, through Jesus Christ, our Lord. Amen.

The Lord knows who are His. 2 Timothy 2:19

God Knows and We Don't

"Look, Mr. Matson died yesterday," said Mrs. Johnson. She was reading about it in the paper. "You know, the man who used to live on the corner?"

"I remember," said Don. "Dad didn't think he was a good Christian because he wouldn't give any money for a new church."

"Yes, but do you remember what I said?" asked Mrs. Johnson. "Don't judge other people. Only God knows who the Christians are. This story in the paper shows that we were probably wrong about Mr. Matson."

"What does it say?" asked Don.

"It says he had been paying all the expenses of a missionary in Africa," said Mrs. Johnson.

"All the expenses? Then he was giving a lot to God! That must have been at least a thousand dollars a year!" Don figured. "Probably more."

"You see?" said Mrs. Johnson. "We thought Mr. Matson was stingy and didn't love God, but all the while he was giving more money for God's work than most people do."

"We can't ever know how much someone else loved God, can we?" said Don.

"No," said his mother. "You can't even know why Mr. Matson gave what he did. Only the love of Jesus makes a person a Christian."

"Well, then," said Don, a little surprised, "how can anyone know for sure who the Christians are?"

"We can't ever know for sure," said his mother, "but God knows. The Bible says, 'The Lord knows who are His,' and that's what counts."

Questions to ask and answer: What did Mrs. Johnson find out about Mr. Matson when he died? Why was she surprised? What did she tell Don? Why can't we ever know for sure who the Christians are? Who does know?

A Bible reading about doing God's work secretly: Matthew 6:1-4.

Let us bow and pray: Heavenly Father, please forgive us for often trying to be judges of other people. We can't know all that they do or why they do it. Help us to remember that *You* are the Judge of all hearts and that You know who loves You and who doesn't. Please fill our hearts with Your love so that we will love You in many ways, through Jesus Christ, our Lord. Amen.

192

The sacrifice that pleases God
most is a broken spirit. Psalm 51:17

Why the Sheep Were Burned

Jack and Ruth were looking at pictures in a Bible story book. When their father came and took a look, too, Ruth pointed to the picture of an altar some people had made long ago. Smoke was going up from the altar. "What are they burning, Daddy?" she asked.

He told her, "They killed a sheep, and now they are having a church service. After a while they will eat most of the sheep. The part they are burning is called a sacrifice."

"What's a sacrifice, Dad?" asked Jack.

"It was a way of telling God, 'We are sorry that we have done wrong. Somebody must die to pay for our sins. Please let it be this sheep instead of us.'"

"Why did God want people to burn the sheep?" asked Jack.

His dad smiled. "What God really cared about was how

193

the people felt inside. If the people were sorry for their sins and wanted God to forgive them, then God was pleased."

"Like when we are sorry for our sins?" asked Jack.

"Yes," said his dad. "King David said, 'The sacrifice that pleases God most is a broken spirit.' A broken spirit is a willingness to say, 'I was wrong; I have sinned.'

"I know a Bible verse that calls Jesus the Lamb of God," said Ruth. " 'Behold the Lamb of God that takes away the sin of the world.' "

"Good girl," said her father. "The sheep sacrifices were only reminders that God would send His Son Jesus to die for all sins."

"Is that why we don't burn sheep in our church services?" asked Jack.

"Right," said his father, patting him on the head. "Our Father in heaven never did care just to have sheep burned. What He wants is for us to be sorry about being bad. That's what it means to have a broken spirit. When we say, 'I'm sorry I did wrong,' then we have a broken spirit. And then God gives us His forgiveness and love for the sake of Jesus, who died for us."

Some questions: What did the people in the Bible tell God with their sacrifices? Who was the Lamb of God who died for us? Why did God want the people in the Bible to burn sheep? What did King David say is the sacrifice that pleases God most? What is a broken spirit? For whose sake is God willing to forgive sins?

Bible reading about two brothers and their sacrifices: Genesis 4:1-7.

Our sacrifices of prayer: Dear Lord, our God, please take our prayer instead of a sheep as a way of telling You we are sorry for our sins. Forgive all our sins for Jesus' sake, who died for us; and give us the Holy Spirit so that we will try to live holy lives for You. Amen.

194

Trust in the Lord. Psalm 37:3

On Board a Big Ship

Janice and her mother were crossing the ocean on a big ship. One evening as they walked hand in hand along the deck, her mother said, "You know, I've been thinking. This boat trip is like our life with God. Can you guess some ways in which the two are alike?"

Janice thought a while. "I know," she said. "We're traveling with many other people, and we don't know where we're going, and Jesus is our Captain, and He'll take us where we want to go."

"Now wait a minute," said her mother. "You were mostly right, but don't you know where we're going?"

"Oh, sure," said Janice. "I meant we couldn't find the way by ourselves. We let the Captain steer the ship."

"Very good," said her mother. "Now, in church windows and in picture books God's church sometimes is pictured as a boat. Who is the Captain of that ship?"

"That's easy," said Janice. "Jesus is the Captain of His church."

Janice and her mother kept on walking and thinking. "Could anyone get across the ocean without going on a ship?" Janice's mother asked her?

"Well, they could fly or go on some other boat," said Janice, "but they'd need some kind of ship, and a captain who could take them to the right place."

"They couldn't get there by trying to swim across by themselves?" asked her mother.

"Of course not," said Janice, laughing.

"All right," said the mother. "Let's remember that we cannot get to heaven by ourselves. But Jesus, our Lord,

195

knows the way, and He takes all who are in His ship to their Father in heaven."

"Just as we're going to see Grandfather," said Janice. "And you know what?" said Janice. "Jesus even paid for our way."

"Yes," said her mother, giving Janice a little hug, "and He takes care of us very well on the way. That's why the Bible often tells us to 'trust in the Lord.'"

Let's talk about this: Where were Janice and her mother going? What did they talk about? Can you tell how a boat trip is like life with God? Why can't anyone get to heaven by himself? What did Jesus have to pay for our way to heaven? Why does the Bible often tell us to "trust in the Lord"?

Bible reading for older children and grownups: Psalm 37:3-5.

Our prayer: Dear Jesus, our Captain on the way to heaven, we are glad that we are with You and that You are taking us to see our Father in heaven. Thank You for paying our way. Please keep us from ever leaving You and Your ship, and from trying to get to heaven by ourselves. Help us always to trust in You, for with You we are safe and in good care. Amen.

Rest in the Lord. Wait patiently for Him.
Don't fret. Psalm 37:7

What Patience Means

Betty had smallpox — not just chicken pox, but smallpox, which can be very dangerous. When there are scabs on the pox, children want to scratch them. And when they do, they get little scars that never go away. Pockmarks they're called.

The doctor knew he had to keep Betty from scratching her pocks, so he told her parents to tie mittens on her hands. She wasn't allowed to take off the mittens, and she couldn't get them off easily when she tried. The doctor also said Betty had to stay in a darkened room for a few days to protect her eyes.

Betty didn't like it at all. She fussed and fretted. She wasn't a bit patient. She wanted to go out and play. And where the pocks were healing, Betty wanted to scratch them so badly, she'd stomp her foot and cry and say mean things.

By and by the itching stopped, and the doctor said she was well. The next day she went over to see her friend Sally.

Sally had also gotten the smallpox, but she was still sick. The shade was pulled down, but not tied down. Sally was playing a game of dominoes by herself and seemed happy.

"How come they don't have to tie your mittens on you? How come you don't pull up the shade? How can you just sit here and be happy?" Betty asked Sally.

"Oh, I'm waiting for God's time," said Sally.

"God's time? What's God's time?" asked Betty.

"Well," Sally explained, "Mother told me the itching is God's time for healing the skin. It would be wrong to fret and try to hurry God in what He must do. So I try to wait patiently for the Lord to make me well. I play games or cut out dolls or listen to records."

The Bible says, "Rest in the Lord. Wait patiently for Him. Don't fret." Believe that God loves you, and give God a chance to help you. He always helps His children when they trust Him enough to be patient.

Let's talk about this: How did Betty fret? Why did she fret? Why did Sally act differently? What does the Bible say we should do instead of fretting? Why can we be sure that God will help us if we will wait patiently for Him?

The story of a patient man: Job 1:13-22.

Let's talk to God: Sometimes, dear Lord, we don't understand what You are doing, and we fret instead of waiting patiently for Your help. Please teach us to trust You more, knowing that You make things come out just right when we wait for You. Amen.

There is not a perfect man on earth who does only good and never sins. Ecclesiastes 7:20

A Real Good Man

Greg liked his new Sunday school superintendent very much. "He's a real good man!" said Greg at the supper table. Everybody agreed — except Susie.

"My teacher said nobody is really good," Susie argued. "My teacher said everybody is a sinner."

"Oh, I know that," said Greg. "But we could still call him a good man, the way people talk, couldn't we, Dad?"

"Well, the Bible calls some people good and others wicked," Greg's father pointed out, "but we don't ever want to get the idea that anyone is as good as he ought to be. That wouldn't be true."

"But I still think Mr. Gordon is a very good man, and I'm sure God thinks so too," said Greg.

"All right," said Susie. "But even a superintendent does some wrong things, and so do pastors and dads and moms and everybody."

"Pastors don't," said little Jean. "They work for God and they're holy."

"No, Jean," said her father. "Everybody does wrong things, your daddy, your mommie, and even Pastor Jacobs. That's why we all need God's forgiveness, and that's why we need to forgive each other all the time. The Bible says, 'There is not a perfect man on earth who does only good and never sins.' "

"But I still think Mr. Gordon is a good man," Greg insisted.

"Sure he is," said Greg's father. "But he's also a sinner.

Mr. Gordon knows this and appreciates God's forgiveness. That's why he loves Jesus and does good things for Him."

Questions to talk about: What did Greg say about the superintendent? Why did Susie say he wasn't good? Who was right? Why do we need to know that everybody sins? How can anyone get rid of his sins? Why was the superintendent good to the children?

Bible reading about a good man: Job 1:1-5.

Our prayer: O Lord, our God, we know that we are all sinners and that nobody but You is really good unless You make him good. Please take away our sins for Jesus' sake, and give us the Holy Spirit so that we will want to be good. In Jesus' name we ask it. Amen.

Jesus paid for our sins, and not for ours only,
but also for the sins of the whole world. 1 John 2:2

Can God Forgive a Murderer?

In the paper one evening there were pictures of a young man who had killed several people.

"God will punish him, won't He?" said Donna. She sounded as though she hoped God would.

"That depends on whether the man wants God's forgiveness," said her mother.

"You mean he could kill someone and ask God to forgive him and then kill another person and be forgiven."

"If he really was sorry both times. But if he *was* really sorry the first time, he would not ever wish to kill again. When we ask God to forgive us and we really mean it, we don't ever want to do that sin again."

"But how can God forgive a person who murders other

people?" asked Donna. She just couldn't believe it was possible.

"Well," her mother answered, "it's only because of what Jesus did for all of us. The Bible says, 'Jesus paid for our sins, and not for ours only, but also for the sins of the whole world.' That includes the killings of a murderer."

"Then even the worst sinner in the whole world could get forgiveness from God," Donna decided.

Her mother agreed. "Peter got forgiveness even though he cursed and said he didn't know Jesus. And Judas could have had forgiveness for selling Jesus if he had asked Jesus for it. So why don't we say a prayer for the young killer and ask God to change his heart?" Donna's mother suggested.

So together they prayed for the young man whose picture was in the paper, and that night Donna's mother marked some salvation verses in a little Gospel of John booklet and wrote on the cover, "We prayed for you. Please read this." The next day she sent the booklet to the killer in jail.

Questions to help us think: What did Donna think would happen to the killer whose picture was in the paper? What didn't Donna believe at first? Why is God willing to forgive even a murderer? Who can say the Bible verse? What did Donna and her mother do for the killer? Why did Donna's mother send him the Gospel of John booklet?

Bible reading: James 5:16-20.

Our prayer: Dear Father in heaven, please keep us from ever doing any great sin. But if it should happen, help us to remember that Jesus paid for all sins. Forgive us our sins, whatever they are, for Jesus' sake, and make us willing to tell others about Your great love in Christ Jesus, our Savior. Amen.

*Be babies in badness, but in thinking
be grown up.* 1 Corinthians 14:20

How Grown Up Are You?

"Aw, he wouldn't know how," said one of the boys who was trying to get Fred to steal some cap guns for them in the dime store. Fred was acting as though he didn't understand what they wanted him to do. Finally he said to them, "It isn't right to steal."

"Well, listen to the little Sunday school teacher talking," said one of the boys, who was trying to act big. "You gonna go tell your mamma?"

Fred didn't let the boys frighten him into doing something wrong. "I don't care what you think," he said. "I'd rather be right with God."

The Bible says, "Be babies in badness, but in thinking be grown up." Fred didn't mind being called a baby for not wanting to steal. He was being a man in thinking the way he did.

The devil gets people to think they are more grown up when they do wrong than when they do what is right and good. But the person who is grown up in his thinking knows how foolish it is to sin and how much better it is to obey God.

Jesus, God's Son, was a real man. The Bible says, "He did no sin." People who keep Him in their hearts become babies in badness but grown up in their thinking.

Questions to help us think: Why did the boys in the gang think that Fred was a sissy? Why wasn't Fred ashamed to be called a baby? Who can repeat the Bible verse from memory? In what way should we be babies? What kind of thinking is grown-up thinking? How can we become grown-up in Christian thinking?

Bible reading: 1 Peter 4:1-5.

Our prayer: Dear Lord, our God, please keep us from growing up in badness. Help us to be grown-up Christians so that we will understand and gladly follow Your ways, through Jesus Christ, our Savior. Amen.

I trusted in You, O Lord. I said,
"You are my God." Psalm 31:14

Putting On Our Life Belt

There was a big hole in the front of the ship. It had run into another boat. When the captain saw that the ship would soon sink, he shouted, "Everybody get a life belt!"

The kind of life belts they had were like a round lifesaver candy, with a hole in the middle. These life belts are big enough to go around your chest. They are made of cork and will keep a person from sinking under the water.

A boy on the top deck stood holding his life belt and shivering with fear. "Put it on," shouted the captain. "It won't do you a bit of good if you don't get into it."

"I don't think it can help me," said the boy. "Maybe

it'll pull me down." He didn't trust the belt, so he didn't want to put on the thing that could save his life.

Just then the mate, a big, strong fellow, came by. He grabbed the belt out of the boy's hand and pushed it over his head and arms, where it belonged. "There," said the mate, "now you'll float when the ship goes down."

The Bible says, "Believe on the Lord Jesus Christ, and you will be saved." Some people don't see how believing in Jesus can save them. They don't trust in Jesus. They don't take Him for their Savior. And so they may go down into hell, which is much worse than going down and dying in water.

"Put on the Lord Jesus Christ," St. Paul told the Romans. Jesus is like a life saver. We must put Him on by trusting that He can save us from our sins and their punishment.

Like the mate, we also need to help other people. We ought to do whatever we can to get others to trust in Jesus, their Savior. With the psalm writer we say, "I trusted in You, O Lord. I said, 'You are my God.'" Other people need to say that, too, in order to be saved.

Questions to talk about: What did the captain tell everyone to do on his ship? Why didn't one boy do it? How did the mate help save the boy's life? In what way is Jesus like a life belt? In what way are some people like the boy who didn't put on his life belt? Who can say what the psalm writer said about trusting the Lord? How can we get others to say this and mean it?

Bible reading: Psalm 32:5-11.

Our prayer: We are trusting You, Lord Jesus, to take care of us here on earth and when we leave for heaven. Make us more willing to help other people to trust in You so that they, too, will be saved. Amen.

Do not lie to one another. Colossians 3:9

To Tell the Truth

"What's a lie?" the teacher in a Christian school asked his class.

"Something that isn't true," said Martin.

"Like a fairy tale or a parable?" asked the teacher.

"No," said Martin, "that wouldn't be a lie. A lie is — I don't know. What *is* a lie?" he asked, looking around at the rest of the class.

"You have to want to cheat people or hurt them," said Edith. "Then it's a lie."

"Like when you say, 'I'll come over right away,' but you don't mean it, that's a lie," said Kathy.

"Or if you say that something you want to sell is good when you know it isn't," said Jane.

"Or even if you say, 'Jim told a lie,' and you think he did, but he didn't," said Allan.

"Or when you say that all people go to heaven and don't need Jesus to save them, that's maybe the worst lie of all," said Ted.

"Well," said the teacher, "now you see that lying is hurting people by not telling the truth, and it's especially bad when you know better and tell lies on purpose. God says in the Bible, 'Do not lie to one another.' And what is our reason for not wanting to?"

All the children knew that answer and raised their hands. "We belong to Jesus and want to be like Him, and He doesn't lie," said John.

"And because we love Jesus, we don't want to hurt other people," added the teacher.

Questions to talk about: Why isn't a fairy tale a lie even though it didn't happen? What is a lie? When is a lie especially bad? What were some of the lies the children mentioned? What does the Bible verse say about lying? What are the main reasons why good Christians do not want to tell lies?

Bible reading: Colossians 3:9-15.

Our prayer: Father in heaven, please forgive us all the lies with which we have hurt people. Help us to speak the truth in love and to follow Jesus also in this way. In His name we ask it. Amen.

Don't swear at all. . . . Let what you say
be just "Yes" or "No." Matthew 5:34, 37

When "Yes" and "No" Are Enough

"I'll bring it right back," said Joe. "Cross my heart and hope to die." He was promising to bring Billy Winter's new bicycle back as soon as he had tried it.

Mr. Winter was standing near Joe and heard what he said.

"Joe," said Mr. Winter, "when you promise to bring something back, we believe you. You don't have to cross your heart and hope to die."

"Is it wrong to say that?" asked Joe. He could tell Mr. Winter didn't like it.

"Well," said Mr. Winter, "would you like to hear what Jesus said about it?"

"Sure," said Joe, so Mr. Winter took out his little New Testament from his pocket and turned to Matthew 5:37. There he read, "Don't swear at all. . . . Let what you say be 'Yes' or 'No.' "

"You see," said Mr. Winter, "even long ago people said 'By heavens' or 'By Jerusalem.' But Jesus said, 'Don't do it. Just say *Yes* or *No*.' If people won't believe you when you just say 'Yes,' then they won't believe you when you say 'Yes, by Jiminy' or 'Cross my heart.' "

"One of our neighbors says 'By Jove.' Is that wrong?" asked Bill.

"That isn't God's name," said Mr. Winter. "But I think our Lord Jesus likes it better if we don't add anything to back up what we say."

So let's remember that Jesus said, "Don't swear at all. Let what you say be 'Yes' or 'No.' " Otherwise we may soon be using God's name without thinking of what we are saying.

Questions to think about: What did Joe say when he promised to return Billy Winter's bike? What did Jesus say about swearing? How did He say we should answer people? Why does Jesus want us to say just "Yes" and "No" without adding something to make it sound more honest and true?

Bible reading: Matthew 5:33-37.

Let us pray: Dear Father in heaven, please help us to watch our talk so that we won't say things that may be wrong. Make us careful to say only words that are helpful, kind, and good, as Jesus would. In His name we ask it. Amen.

The way of a fool is right in his own eyes,
but a wise man listens to advice. Proverbs 12:15

Pigheaded Pete

We shouldn't call people names like "Pigheaded Pete," but in a way Peter Martin deserved his nickname.

"I think you'd better wear a jacket. It's cool outside," his mother would say. "Aw, I don't need a jacket," Peter would argue. So he'd go outside and freeze.

"Write your 5 this way," the teacher told Pete, and showed him how. "I want to do it my way," he would say, and kept on writing it backwards.

Peter was foolish to think he was always right. He was foolish in being stubborn. The Bible says, "The way of a fool is right in his own eyes, but a wise man listens to advice." We can learn much when we listen to others.

That's true most of all when we do wrong. If somebody tells us, "What you are doing is a sin," we ought to be willing to stop and think. If it's true, we ought to change our behavior. Only in that way will we learn God's ways. But nobody learns by being pigheaded or stubborn.

Some people would rather be wrong than corrected. The Bible calls such a person a fool. A wise person thinks over what other people tell him. A wise person listens to advice.

208

You see, sometimes other people are right. They're always right when they tell us the Word of God.

The biggest fool is the person who thinks His ways are all right and doesn't believe that he needs God's forgiveness and help. The wise man believes the Word of God and asks Jesus to be his Savior and Helper.

Questions to think about: What did some people call Peter Martin? How did he get that name? Why is it foolish to think that your way is always right? What does the Bible call a person who listens to advice? What advice does God give people who admit they have done wrong and want His forgiveness?

Bible reading for older children and grownups: Psalm 119:9-12.

Our prayer: Dear Lord, please keep us from ever thinking that we are always right and cannot be wrong. Make us wise enough to learn from other people and especially from those who teach us Your Word, that we may be Your dear children through Jesus Christ, and gladly follow His ways. Amen.

Through love help one another. Galatians 5:13

The Best Neighbors

"I wonder why the new neighbors are so friendly," said Mr. Stone. Mr. Stone was a rich man, and people were always asking him for money or for favors. "Nobody does anything for nothing," he said.

But these new neighbors never asked for anything. They were always giving him something or were trying to help him.

One day the Stones came home late from a trip. They had nothing much to eat in the house. The neighbor woman noticed it and brought over some soup and pie and some homemade bread and some cheese. The Stones were very pleased.

When the Stones' little grandson came to visit but was afraid to stay alone with the maid, the neighbors kept him overnight.

The next day Mr. Stone asked, "What's your charge?" The neighbors laughed at him. There was no charge. They enjoyed helping people.

It took quite a while, but at last Mr. Stone found out why his neighbors were kind. They were churchgoing people. They believed in Jesus and had God's love in their hearts. This love made them want to help others. He thought they were the best neighbors he could have.

So when the new neighbors started talking to Mr. Stone about Jesus in the back yard one evening, he listened. He even told his wife about the talk later that night. They decided they needed God's love in their hearts and home, too.

The Bible says, "Through love help one another." We Christians can be the kindest, friendliest, happiest, best people on earth because Jesus helps us to be so. His law is summed up in one sentence: "You are to love your neighbor as yourself." When His love is in our hearts, that's what we want to do.

Questions to talk about: Why did Mr. Stone think his neighbors were friendly? Why *were* they friendly? How did their love help them to share Jesus with the Stone family? Why can Christians be the happiest and best neighbors? Who can say a Bible verse about loving others?

A Bible reading that describes love: 1 Corinthians 13:4-7. Read "love" when it says "charity."

210

Our prayer: O Lord of Love, please forgive the times we have been unfriendly and unkind. Help us always to act as children of Your great love, which we receive through Christ Jesus, our Savior. Amen.

Bless the Lord, O my soul, and forget not all His benefits. Psalm 103:2

What Jim Didn't Remember

Jim had a toothache. He prayed to God to make the toothache go away. The next morning it was gone, so Jim didn't think about it any more. He even forgot that he had asked God to help him. And, of course, he didn't thank God.

The next day was Jim's birthday. "Please let me have a dog for a pet, dear God," he prayed that morning. He didn't get a dog, but he got two pretty white rabbits. "I like them even better than a dog," said Jim. But he forgot that God is the Giver of all good gifts, and so he forgot to thank God.

Two days later Jim got into some grease in the garage. His mother had told him to stay away from the motor his dad was fixing. "Please, God," Jim prayed, "help me to clean this off my clothes so Mother won't get angry."

Jim didn't get the grease off his clothes, but his mother didn't get angry. She only said, "Jimmy, please help me by being more careful with your clothes." As usual, Jim forgot about his prayer, and he also didn't thank God for a mother who was kind and forgiving.

On Sunday the teacher in Sunday school asked, "Do any of you remember how God answered your prayers this past week?" Some did. But Jim said, "I don't think God ever answered any of my prayers."

Jim didn't know how God had answered his prayers. Do you see why? He forgot how he had prayed. He also forgot to thank God for his blessings. That's why he didn't know how God answered his prayers.

The psalm writer said, "Bless the Lord, O my soul, and forget not all His benefits." We ought to thank Him especially for His loving Spirit and His forgiveness of all our sins. For Jesus' sake He gladly gives His love every day to all who ask Him. So "bless the Lord, O my soul, and forget not all His benefits."

Questions to talk about: What were some of the prayers Jimmy prayed? How did God answer these? Why didn't Jimmy notice that God answered his prayers? What does the psalm verse tell us not to forget? For what special gifts ought we to thank God every day?

A prayer promise: Matthew 7:7-11.

Let us pray: Dear God, please forgive the many times we forget to thank You for what You do for us. Help us to notice Your ways of blessing us so that we will love and praise You more than we do. In Jesus' name we ask this. Amen.

We, though many, are one body in Christ. Romans 12:5

One Big Happy Family

The Nelson family bought a farm in Iowa. Soon after they moved to their new home, the neighbors came to welcome them. All the neighbors were nice people, but especially the Millers seemed like old friends right from the start.

"I'm glad to see that picture of Jesus on your wall," said Mrs. Miller. "We believe in Him, too, so that makes us relatives. Have you joined a church? We'll be glad to have you come to ours."

When everybody was gone, Mrs. Nelson said to her husband, "Isn't it wonderful how quickly we feel at home with people who believe in Jesus as we do?"

"I was thinking the same thing," said Mr. Nelson. "It's like the time I was in the Army. I was always glad to find someone else who was a real Christian. The love of Jesus draws His followers together."

"We learned a Bible verse about that in Sunday school once," said Beverly. She meant the verse: "We, though many, are one body in Christ." The church of Jesus is like

213

our body. It has many members or parts, but they're all connected to one head. Jesus is the Head of His body of followers.

"When people are Christians, you know a whole lot about them right away," said Mr. Nelson. "You know they love God and pray and want to be honest, and, oh, so many other things. You really do feel related, like brothers and sisters in a big happy family."

"That's why we also want to worship and work together with other Christians here on earth," Mrs. Nelson added. "So where do you think we're all going Sunday?" she asked, as though she didn't know.

Questions to ask: What did Mrs. Miller notice on the wall of the Nelson home? Why did the Nelsons and the Millers feel like old friends? What had Beverly learned about the church of Jesus? What are some of the things we know about people who are really Christians? Where do you think the Nelson family went the next Sunday?

Bible reading: 1 Corinthians 12:12-27.

Our prayer: Lord Jesus, we are glad that You have made us members of Your body. Help us remember that all who believe in You are children of God and our brothers and sisters. Please add many more people to Your church so that they, too, may enjoy Your love and blessings as we do. Amen.

We brought nothing into this world, and it is certain we can carry nothing out. 1 Timothy 6:7

What Good Is Money?

An old lady lived all alone in New York. She was very, very rich, but she hid all her money and never used it to help anybody, not even herself.

One day the old woman died because she didn't even buy enough food for herself. Her neighbors paid for her funeral. They thought she was very poor.

When the police searched the woman's house, they opened a chest of drawers. It was full of money and bank papers. In a closet they found some boxes full of money.

What good did it do the woman to have so much money? Her relatives got it all when she died.

The Bible tells us, "We brought nothing into this world, and it is certain we can carry nothing out." What God gives us for just a while He wants us to use in good ways. When God gives us more than we need, He wants us to help others. Money is good to have when we use it for what we need and for helping others.

Children as well as grownups need to learn how money should be used. Some people love money. Some waste it. We must remember that our money or anything else we have is given to us by God only for a short time and that it is to be used for good reasons. Then we have the secret of how to enjoy God's gifts.

God also wants us to be satisfied and happy with what He gives us. We can be happy when Jesus is in our heart, because then we know that God loves us, no matter what He gives us.

Questions to think about: Why did the old lady die? What good did her money do her? What are some wrong ways of using money? What does God want us to do with the money He gives us? What does our Bible verse say about money and other things we own? Why can we be happy with whatever God gives us?

Bible reading: Matthew 6:19-21.

Our prayer: Forgive us, dear heavenly Father, for often wanting to keep things selfishly for ourselves. Help us to see how You want us to use our money and things, and make us glad to use them in ways that are pleasing to You. We ask this in Jesus' name. Amen.

Train up a child in the way
he should go. Proverbs 22:6

God's Baby Sitters

"Mommy, you must be God's baby sitter," said little Susie.

"What makes you think so?" asked her mother.

"Well, when Mrs. Hanson comes and takes care of me, she's your baby sitter. So when you take care of me, you're God's baby sitter, aren't you?"

Susan's mother agreed. "In a way, you're right," she

216

said. "You are really God's child. Your daddy and I are just taking care of you for God a little while."

"You're my best baby sitter," said Susie as she gave her mother a hug.

"I'm glad you like me," said her mother. "What do you think God's baby sitter ought to do for Him?"

"Hm," said Susie. After thinking hard, she went on: "A baby sitter shouldn't let us do anything wrong. A good baby sitter keeps an eye on us and also tells us what you want us to do. And we like it when she reads to us or plays and sings with us."

"Very good," said her mother, who was beginning to enjoy the idea of being a baby sitter for God. "I sometimes leave a note for your baby sitters. Do you know where God's notes are for His baby sitters?"

"Sure," said Susie. "They're in the Bible. Is that why you read your Bible so often?" she asked.

"That's one reason," said Susie's mother. "Do you know what one of God's notes said to me last week? 'Train up a child in the way he should go.' What do you think that way is?" she asked.

"It's the way Jesus wants me to go," said Susie. "It's going with Him."

And that was right. The Christian way is the way God wants us to go.

Questions to answer: What did little Susie call her mother? Why did she think that? What are some of the things a good baby sitter does? What does God want parents to do for Him? Where did Susie's mother find her notes from God? What was the Bible note she told Susie?

Bible reading: Matthew 18:1-6.

Our prayer: Please, dear God, give everyone in our house the love of Jesus so that we will grow up loving Him and following Your ways, through Jesus Christ, our Lord. Amen.

217

Jesus is the One chosen by God to be the Judge of the living and the dead. Acts 10:42

When the Judge Is Your Friend

"And don't you ever do that again," said the angry policeman, "or I'll bring you before Judge Horn, and he'll be rough with you." Most policemen are friendly, but this one wasn't.

Danny was sorry he had crossed the street when the light was red, but he said to himself, "The judge won't be rough with me; he comes to our house often, and he's my friend."

Danny was sure the judge would be kind to him because Judge Horn was his friend. That's why he wasn't afraid of the judge, and that's why the policeman's words didn't frighten him the way they would have otherwise.

The Bible says, "Jesus is the One chosen by God to be the Judge of the living and the dead." Jesus is the Ruler of the world. He is the One who will decide whether or not a person must be punished for what he does wrong. He is the Judge before whom everybody will have to stand.

But we can say, "I'm not afraid of the Judge. He's my Friend. He's my Savior. He loves me so much that He died for me on a cross."

218

The Judge of the world died to pay for our sins. So He knows that our fines are paid; He paid them Himself. We won't even have to remind Him. Because we want what He did to count for us, He'll forgive us our sins and not punish us as we deserve.

Isn't that a good thing to know? Even the devil can't scare us when Jesus, our Judge, is our Friend. Let's not forget to thank Jesus for that.

Questions to help us think: How did the policeman try to scare Danny? Why was Danny sure the judge would be kind to him? Who will be the Judge of all people at the end of the world? How do we know that the Judge will be kind and forgiving to us? Why won't we have to pay for what we have done wrong? How can we show that we appreciate the Judge's love and friendship?

Bible reading for older children and grownups: Romans 8:31-34.

Our prayer: Dear Jesus, we are glad that You are not only our Judge but also our loving Savior and Friend. Please judge us as your friends and not as we deserve to be judged. Have mercy on us, dear Jesus, forgive us all our sins, and help us to praise and serve You forever in love. Amen.

Jesus has made us clean
from our sins. Revelation 1:5

How We Are Washed by Jesus

"Mommie, do I have to be washed in blood?" said little four-year-old Janice when she came home from Sunday school.

"Why, no," said her mother. "Whoever told you that?"

"My Sunday school teacher," said Janice. "She wants us to be washed in Jesus' blood."

Bobby, her older brother, snickered, but his father shook his head at him. Then he said to Janice, "Your teacher didn't mean that you had to be washed with blood the way we wash with water. She meant that you had to let Jesus wash away your sins the way water washes away dirt."

"But how can He do that with His blood?" asked Janice.

"When Jesus died on a cross," said her father, "His blood ran out of His hands and His feet and His side. But He gave His blood for us. This means that He gave His life for us. He died for us. When we believe this, we get God's forgiveness."

"But why did Jesus have to die for us?" asked Janice.

"Well, you see, Janice," he said, "we have all kinds of wrong thoughts and feelings. We're not the kind of people God wants us to be. Jesus died on a cross so that we could have forgiveness and a new life from God."

"See the dirt on this potato?" said Janice's mother. "Now I'll wash it with water. See, it's clean. The water took the dirt away. The Bible says, 'The blood of Jesus . . . cleanses us from all sin.'"

When we believe that Jesus died for us and is our Lord and Savior, God forgives our sins. That's why the Bible also says, "Jesus has made us clean from our sins by His blood."

220

Janice didn't understand all of that just yet, but by and by she understood it better; and she loved Jesus for being her Savior and thanked Him for taking her sins away.

Questions to talk about: What did the teacher tell Janice? What did Janice think this meant? What does it really mean? Why did Jesus give us His blood and life on a cross? For how many sins did Jesus pay?

Bible reading for older children and adults: Hebrews 9:11-15.

Our prayer: Lord Jesus, we owe You so much for giving Your blood and Your life for us! Please wash away all our sins, and give us the Holy Spirit so that we will also live a clean and good life for You. Amen.

Whoever breaks one of the least important commandments of God and teaches others to do so will be called small in the kingdom of heaven. But whoever teaches and does them will be called great in the kingdom of heaven. Matthew 5:19

Little Things That Matter

"Aw, who cares?" said Karen when her mother asked her to pick up the paper dolls on the living-room floor. "Nobody's coming."

Karen's mother stopped her ironing. "I care," she said, "and I'm sure God cares. God wants you to obey your parents in little things as well as in big things."

"But, Mother," Karen argued, "what's the difference whether I do it now or afterwhile?"

"The difference," said her mother, "is in your spirit. You see, with God little things sometimes matter the most. The

221

person who obeys God in little things usually loves Him more than people who do just the big things."

So caring about God in little things is very important. That's what Jesus was trying to teach us when He said, "Whoever breaks one of the least important commandments of God and teaches others to do so will be called small in the kingdom of heaven. But whoever teaches and does them will be called great in the kingdom of heaven."

Sometimes people think it doesn't matter if we sin just a little. Or they think some of the things God has told us are not important. Remember, it is often in the little things we do that we show how little or how much we love Him.

That's why Karen's mother was very happy when Karen picked up her paper dolls and put them away neatly.

Questions to talk about: What did Karen think didn't matter? What did her mother tell her? Who will be called great in God's kingdom? What are some little ways in which we can show our love to God?

Bible reading: Matthew 5:17-20.

Let us pray: Lord Jesus, please forgive us for not caring enough about what God's will is. Make us willing to please you also in the little things that don't seem important. Help us to show our love for You in all that we do, also in the little things. Amen.

*Jesus said to His Father, "Not My will,
but Yours, be done." Luke 22:42*

We Might Be Wrong

Billy and his sisters were having their first dinner in a restaurant. Billy looked at the card. He didn't know what all the words meant.

"I think this looks good," he said to the waiter. "But don't bring it if it isn't good."

"Me, too," said his sister Susan. "Bring me what's good."

So they left it up to the waiter to bring what he thought was best. And they enjoyed very much what he brought. He even made them a pink lemonade for a surprise.

In a way, that's how we ought to let God do things for us. We don't know what is really good for us. So the best we can do is to let God decide. God's will is always better than our will because He knows so much more than we do. And we could be wrong.

Even when it meant dying on a cross, Jesus said to His Father in heaven, "Not My will, but Yours, be done." Jesus knew that He must suffer to save people from sin and hell. Jesus also taught His disciples to pray, "Our Father, who art in heaven . . . Thy will be done."

Whenever we let God decide what should be done, He does what is best for us. So even though God tells us to ask Him for whatever we want, it's always better to add, "but please do what You think is best."

Questions to talk about: Why did the children let the waiter decide their order? How did that work out? How did Jesus pray to His Father in heaven? Why did He teach us to pray, "Thy will be done"? Why aren't we always willing to let God decide things for us? How do all things turn out when we let God decide what should happen?

Bible reading: Matthew 26:36-44.

Let us bow and pray: Lord Jesus, teach us to pray as You did, and to trust our Father in heaven. Help us to believe that all things work out good for them that love God, because our Father in heaven loves us for Your sake. Amen.

There is great profit in living with God and being satisfied. 1 Timothy 6:6

How to Make a Great Profit

Do you know what a profit is?

Larry's dad bought a car for $500 and sold it for $600. He made a profit of $100. Grace's father received money for working in a factory. That was his profit. Mr. Miller was a farmer. He made some money by feeding cattle. What he gained was his profit.

Nearly everybody wants to profit by what he does. We all want to make some money or get some good out of what we do.

Some people want to make big profits fast so they can buy a big house and a new car and lots of fancy clothes and the best food. Some people even cheat to get money and things that money can buy.

There is a better way to make a great profit. It's a sure way of getting a good and happy life. The Bible says: "There is great profit in living with God and being satisfied."

There is a famous doctor who could be a rich man living in a big home. But he gives his time and money to a hospital in the jungles of Africa. He is satisfied with a small house and very little pay for himself because he loves God and wants to help the African people.

A nurse who lives in New Guinea could get good wages and a husband in America, but she went to New Guinea to help the people there because she loves God. God will make her happier than she would be if she received much money. He will bless her much in other ways.

"There is great profit in living with God and being satisfied." Those who are satisfied with having God's love and life with Him through faith in Jesus get the most out of life on earth. And think of the wonderful life with God they get in heaven!

Questions: What is meant by great profit? What does the Bible say is the best way to get a great profit? Why can we be satisfied and happy when Jesus is our Friend and Savior? What are some of the profits that come from being satisfied with God's love?

Bible reading: Acts 4:32-37.

Our prayer: Lord God, our Father in heaven, please make us completely satisfied with the love which You give through Jesus Christ, our Lord. Give us the Holy Spirit so that we will believe that there is great profit in loving You and will find joy in serving You. In Jesus' name we ask it. Amen.

Now is the day of salvation. 2 Corinthians 6:2

Our Time Is Now

Lorna took her little neighbor boy Bobby to Sunday school and church with her every Sunday. But often Lorna had to wait for Bobby to get ready. While she waited she would talk to his daddy or mother and invite them to church, too.

"We'll come sometime," Bobby's dad would say. But he didn't really mean it. "Maybe when we're older and haven't so much to do," said Bobby's mother.

One Sunday morning a man was at Bobby's house, trying to sell some insurance. Lorna listened while she waited for Bobby to get ready.

"There's lots of time for me to take out insurance," said Bobby's dad. "I'm still young."

"Let me tell you something," said the agent. "Yesterday one of my friends died. He was only 25 years old. He thought he would get to be 80. But nobody knows. We ought to be ready."

"That's right," said Lorna, before she even knew what she was saying.

"Lorna's our neighbor girl," said Bobby's dad. "She's been telling me to go to church. I say there's plenty of time for such things, but you say there isn't. Do you go?" he asked the insurance man.

"Well, no, but I guess a person should," he said. It made him think. Lorna never heard about it, but that man started going to church a few weeks later.

While we are living on earth, God offers to forgive our sins and to adopt us as His children for Jesus' sake. Let's not ever think our life with God can be put off until later. We don't know how long God will let us live. Tomorrow may be too late because tomorrow may never come. Our time is NOW. The Bible says,"Now is the day of salvation."

Questions to talk about: What did Lorna tell Bobby's folks one Sunday? What did they say? What did the insurance man tell about his young friend? What does God mean when He says, "Now is the day of salvation"?

Bible reading for good readers: 2 Corinthians 6:1, 2, 16-18.

Our prayer: Dear Lord, our God, please keep us from ever wanting to wait till some other time to be Your children. Make us glad that NOW is our chance to have Your love. Help us to find ways of telling others that NOW is the time to live with Jesus in His kingdom. Amen.

Go to the ant, lazy-bones; watch her ways
and be wise. Proverbs 6:6

What the Ants Teach Us

"Why do I have to do the dishes? Bob doesn't!" Leona complained as she sat reading a book.

"Bob cuts the lawn and keeps the weeds out of the flowers," said her mother.

"I'll trade you, Sis," said Bob. "But then you'll have to do everything I do."

Leona wasn't sure she wanted to, because Bob always kept himself busy. She quit grumbling, but still she wasn't a bit happy as she helped clear the table.

Leona's mother worried about her laziness. "Everybody needs to learn to work," her mother told her. "I hope you will learn to like work. Your life won't amount to much if you don't enjoy working."

"Like work?" asked Leona. She seemed surprised that anyone could enjoy working.

"You oughta watch my ants," said Bob. "They're happy because they're busy. You'd be happier, too, if you weren't so lazy."

Bob had a little ant colony in a glass box on the back porch. His mother said, "Yes, the Bible tells us to go and watch how hard the ants work. They teach us not to be lazy."

Leona took a good look at those ants hurrying to carry food or sand from one place to another. "Those ants certainly are busy," she said. "I guess God wants us to work."

"You can be sure of that," said her mother. "Even Jesus worked hard, and He wouldn't have had to."

"That's why I want to be a carpenter," said Bob.

"Why not be a church teacher like I'm gonna be?" said

Leona. "Jesus was a teacher, you know; and teaching God's Word is *God's* work!"

The Bible says, "*Whatever* your hand finds to do, do it with your might." The ants are a good example of hard workers. That's why the Bible says, "Go to the ant, lazybones; watch her ways and be wise."

Questions to talk about: Why was Leona's mother worried about her? Why did she want Leona to learn to work? What did her brother Bob tell her to watch? What does the Bible say we should learn from the ant? How did Leona show that she planned to work for God?

Bible reading about laziness: Proverbs 6:6-11.

Our prayer: Lord God, please forgive our laziness and keep us from being lazy. Help us to enjoy work as well as play, and teach us to do our work for You. We ask this in the name of Jesus, who never got tired of working for others. Amen.

It is more blessed to give than to receive. Acts 20:35

More Fun Than Getting

"Why, Johnny, what's the matter?" asked his mother. "Why are you crying? I thought all these Christmas presents from your friends at school would make you happy."

Johnny had TB and wasn't allowed to get out of bed. His class at school had sent him a big sack of packages.

"I *am* happy to get all these presents," said Johnny, "but I wish I could go to school and give somebody else a present."

Johnny knew that "it is more blessed to give than to receive," just as Jesus said. So he and his mother planned to send a big box of cookies to his friends. And he got more fun out of that than out of the presents he received.

What made Johnny even happier was planning to give Jesus a present. "After all, Christmas is Jesus' birthday," said Johnny. "He gave His life for me, so I want to give Him a present."

Most children haven't learned what Johnny knew. They think they'll be happy only by getting things. "I want this" and "Can't I have that?" and "Gimme some more," they keep on saying. But often the children who get the most are the least happy.

Children who learn to know Jesus learn to love; and those who love to give are much happier than those who only want to get. Let's remember what Jesus said, "It is more blessed to give than to receive." That's true.

Questions to talk about: What did Jesus say was better than getting presents? What was Jesus glad to give us? What made Him glad to give His life? What was Johnny glad to give Jesus? Why?

Bible reading: Acts 20:32-35.

Our prayer: Dear Jesus, please help us to believe that "it is more blessed to give than to receive." Give us the Holy Spirit so that we will enjoy Your love also by sharing it with others. Amen.

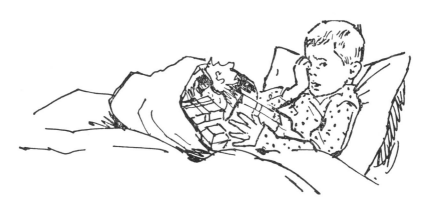

*Put away all . . . dirty talk out
of your mouth.* Colossians 3:8

Where to Put Dirty Talk

The man was dressed in a clean white suit and looked nice. But when he spoke, dirty, rotten, bad words came out of his mouth.

God wouldn't care much if the man's clothes were dirty, but He does care about dirty talk. In the Bible He says, "Put away all . . . dirty talk out of your mouth." A person who talks dirty is dirty in his thinking.

Often children like to say dirty words. They think that such words are funny. Some older boys and girls even think that saying rotten words makes them big and tough.

One day a boy was caught writing dirty words on a toilet wall. His teacher was very much surprised because the boy said he was a Christian. "How can you keep such thoughts inside of you and expect Jesus to stay in your heart?" asked the teacher.

The boy didn't want to answer. He knew he would have to ask Jesus to take away the dirtiness out of his mind and mouth if he wanted Jesus to stay in his heart. Because he loved Jesus, the boy said, "I'm sorry and I'm ashamed of what I did. I'll wash off what I wrote."

"And don't forget to ask Jesus to forgive you for what you did," said the teacher. "He'll be glad to keep you from ever doing such a thing as this again."

The apostle Paul told the Christians in Corinth that God said: "I will be a Father to you, and you shall be My sons and daughters." Then he wrote, "Since we have these promises, let us clean ourselves from all dirtiness." This includes putting away all dirty talk out of our mouths.

Let's talk about this: Why is a clean mouth more important than clean clothes? Why do some children like to say or write dirty words? Why was the teacher surprised to find one of his boys writing dirty words on a toilet wall? What did the teacher ask the boy? Why didn't the boy want to answer? How did he get forgiveness for his sin? How can we put away dirty talk?

Bible reading for older children and grownups: Colossians 3:1-8.

Let us pray: Create in me a clean heart, O God. Wash away all dirty talk out of my mind and mouth. Please give me more of the Holy Spirit so that I will think only clean and beautiful thoughts, through Jesus Christ, my Lord. Amen.

In everything give thanks. 1 Thessalonians 5:18

A Secret Way to Stay Happy

When Roberta broke Janet's doll, Janet didn't say one angry word. "Aren't you going to get angry, Janet?" Roberta asked, quite surprised.

"No, I have a secret way of staying happy," said Janet. "I learned it from my mother. No matter what happens, I think of the good things I have. When I think of them, I thank God for them. Then I don't feel so bad about what I don't have."

232

Janet's mother heard what she was saying and was surprised. "I didn't know Janet got that secret from me," she said. "I found it in the Bible."

"Could I see it in the Bible?" asked Roberta.

"Yes," said Janet's mother. Then she got her Bible to show Roberta where the verse was. She had it marked with red crayon so she could quickly see it when she came to that page. It said, "In everything give thanks, because this is the will of God in Christ Jesus for you."

"Does God really want us to give thanks even when bad things happen?" Roberta asked. "Do you think He wants us to be thankful because I broke the doll?"

"Maybe not because you broke the doll," said Janet's mother, "but because God loves us. He gave us His Son Jesus to save us, and He blesses us with so many other good things. I'm sure He'll see that Janet gets another doll, too."

"I wish I belonged to Jesus," said Roberta, "so I could be happy all the time."

"Oh, now I'm even glad you broke the doll," said Janet. "You can belong to Jesus. If you want Him to be your Savior, He'll take you. And if you'll come to Sunday school and church with me, you'll get to know Him better."

So that's how Janet's friend Roberta learned to know more about Jesus and His love. And by learning more about Jesus, she soon found many reasons to give thanks in everything.

Questions to help us think: What surprised Roberta? What was Janet's secret way of staying happy? Why was Janet able to give thanks in everything? What even made Janet glad that Roberta had broken the doll? Let's all say the Bible verse. Can you think of something bad that turned out good for you?

Bible reading for good readers: Matthew 19:27-30.

Let us pray: Dear Father in heaven, we're glad that You love us and won't let anything happen to us that is really bad. Please help us to remember Your love, also when things go wrong for us. Give us the Holy Spirit so that we will give thanks in everything. In Jesus' name we ask it. Amen.

*Let all that you do be done
in love.* 1 Corinthians 16:14

The Little Wheel That Caused Trouble

Once there was a beautiful little car with four shiny wheels. The four wheels had a good time going places as long as they obeyed the steering wheel and went together.

But one day one of the little wheels decided to do what it wanted to do without caring about the other wheels. When the steering wheel told it to turn right, it turned left. This jerked the other wheels and stopped the car. A truck had to come and take it to a garage.

When the little wheel saw the trouble it had caused, it was sorry and wanted another chance. So after it was straightened out, it didn't think only of itself any more.

234

Instead, it helped the other wheels go where the steering wheel wanted them to go together.

Sometimes we think we may do as we please. When we do so without caring about what happens to others around us, we cause a lot of trouble and usually hurt ourselves, too.

The Bible says, "None of us lives to himself" nor by himself. There are always other people besides us who are hurt or blessed by what we do.

To keep us going places together with those around us, we need a steering wheel. The best steering wheel we can have is Jesus, our Lord and Savior. He tells us in the Bible, "Let all that you do be done in love." Love is caring about the people around us — caring about what will happen to them.

Jesus cared very much about what would happen to us. That is why He obeyed His Father in heaven and even went all the way to the cross for us. Now He wants us to care about others because we have His love in our hearts.

And here's a wonderful secret: Caring about other people makes us happy, too.

Questions for conversation: When did the wheels of the little car roll along happily? What happened when one of the wheels decided to disobey the steering wheel? Who is our steering wheel? How do we know for sure that Jesus loves us very much? What is the main reason we have for loving other people?

Bible reading for older children and adults: Romans 14:7-13.

Let us pray: Dear Father in heaven, forgive us for often causing trouble by not loving and by wanting our own way. Please give us the Holy Spirit so that we will love You and those around us in all that we do. This we ask for the sake of Jesus, who loved us and died for us. Amen.

The fruit of the Spirit
  is in goodness. Ephesians 5:9

The Little Girl's Nicest Gift

On the last day of classes before the Christmas holidays the second grade of Bethel School had a Christmas party. All the children except one brought a present for the teacher. Mary Lou was the only girl who had no present. She was from a very poor family.

As Mary Lou sat and watched the other children take their presents to the teacher, she felt like crying. What would the teacher think of her and, oh, how she wished she had something to give to show her love.

Then she got an idea and marched up to her teacher's desk. "Miss Rowan," she said, "I didn't have any money to buy you a present, but if I'm real good all day, will that be nice enough?"

Miss Rowan looked at little Mary Lou with a smile that went all over her face. "That would be the nicest gift of all," she said, and she meant it.

Mary Lou wanted to give her teacher something because she loved her teacher. We love God because He first loved us and gave us His Son Jesus. Jesus gave His life for us and gives us the Holy Spirit. When we love God, it makes us happy to give Him something.

God is glad to receive our gifts when we love Him. And being good is the nicest gift we can give God to show our love.

God wants us to be good and to do good. He makes us good when Jesus puts the Holy Spirit into our hearts. The Bible says, "The fruit of the Spirit is in goodness." Being good shows that the Holy Spirit is in us.

Let's talk about this: Why did Mary Lou feel like crying at the school Christmas party? What did she ask the teacher? What did the teacher answer? Why do God's children want to give Him gifts? When do our gifts please Him? What is the gift that pleases Him the most?

Bible reading: Ephesians 2:4-10.

Our prayer: Dear Father in heaven, because You are pleased when I am good, make me good and full of good works through Jesus Christ and the Holy Spirit. Amen.

A servant of the Lord must not quarrel
but must be gentle. 2 Timothy 2:24

The Quarrelsome Young Missionary

"I think I'll be a missionary," said Harvey. "I like to argue religion."

"Harvey's good at that," said his sister Ellen. "You should hear him tell Tommy off when Tommy makes fun of going to church."

"Yeah, I gave him a piece of my mind when he said Sunday school was for the birds," Harvey bragged.

"Did you get him to go with you so he'll learn to love Jesus?" asked his father.

"No," Harvey admitted, "I haven't seen him since. He's staying away from me."

"You know," said his father, "maybe you won an argument and lost a boy for Jesus."

"Well," said Harvey, trying to make his arguing seem right, "we're supposed to speak for Jesus, aren't we?"

"Yes," said his father, "but Jesus didn't tell us to be lawyers for Him. Do you know what He said we should be for Him?"

"I know," said Ellen. "He said, 'You shall be My witnesses.'"

"What's the difference?" Harvey argued. "It's all the same."

"No, it isn't," said Ellen. "A lawyer argues; a witness just tells what he knows and believes. He can be real sweet and helpful."

Now their mother spoke up. "I read a verse in the Bible last week that tells us not to argue, especially not in speaking for Jesus," she told them. "It says, 'A servant of the Lord must not strive but must be gentle.' I wrote *quarrel* over the word *strive,* because we know that word better."

"See, Harvey," said his dad, "a missionary mustn't try to win *arguments* but *people.* When we argue too hard, it gets to be quarreling, and then we lose the people."

"All right," said Harvey, "this week I'll try to win Tommy for Jesus by being gentle, and then we'll see."

Was Harvey ever surprised! The night he treated Tommy to a milk shake and told him he was sorry about the way he had talked, Tommy said, "You're okay, Harvey. Guess I'll go to Sunday school with you next Sunday."

238

Questions to talk about: What did Harvey want to be? What did he think missionaries had to do? What's the difference between a lawyer and a witness? What does Jesus want us to be for Him? Why is it better to win a person than an argument? Who can say the Bible verse Harvey's mother found?

Bible reading for good readers: 2 Timothy 2:22-26.

Our prayer: Please forgive our proud quarreling, dear Lord, and help us to be gentle so that we will not win arguments but people for You. For their sakes we ask it, O Lord. Amen.

He who is slow in getting angry is better than the mighty. Proverbs 16:32

How to Become Strong

Billy and Bert were quarreling. Soon they were saying angry words. Then Billy pushed Bert, and Bert hit Billy hard with a fly swatter.

Aunt Sue came into the room and stopped the fighting. "Don't you remember what happened when Cain and Abel quarreled?" she asked them.

"It wasn't Abel's fault," said Billy. He was trying to put the blame on Bert.

"Yeah, but you started this fight, and I'm going to finish it," said Bert, looking very angry.

"Bert," said Aunt Sue kindly, "God warned Cain when he became angry. He told Cain to watch out or he would soon do something real bad. You know what happened. Out in the field Cain became so angry that he took a stone or a club and killed his brother."

239

"Aw, we weren't that angry," said Bert, a little ashamed.

"I hope not," said Aunt Sue. "You won't grow up to be a good husband and a good father unless you learn to keep your temper down."

The Bible says, "He who is slow in getting angry is better than the mighty." In other words, the person who can control his temper is stronger than a great big fighter.

So why don't we ask God to forgive us our bad temper and to give us the power to control it? The Holy Spirit, the Spirit of Jesus, will make us strong in character. He will make us "better than the mighty."

Questions to talk about: To what did Bert and Billy's quarreling lead? Why did Aunt Sue remind them of Cain and Abel? What happened when Cain lost his temper? What does the Bible say about the person who is slow in getting angry? Why is it bad to get angry easily? How do you think we can learn to control our tempers?

Bible reading about Cain and Abel: Genesis 4:3-15.

Our prayer: Dear Father in heaven, please forgive the many times we have gotten angry too quickly. Help us to control our anger at all times so that we will not fall into even greater sins. We ask this in the name of Jesus, our Lord. Amen.

Whoever makes himself small
will be made big. Matthew 23:12

Stooping to Win

"You better watch out for that old man who moved into the house next to you," said David. "He looks mean, and he yells at the kids."

Sure enough, one day Tommy ran too fast around the corner of his house and stepped on one of Mr. Nelson's flowers. Through the window Mr. Nelson saw what happened and came out scolding.

Tommy stopped and came back to talk to Mr. Nelson. Tommy said, "I'm sorry I stepped on your flower. I didn't watch where I was going. I'll ask my dad to plant another flower in its place."

The old man was surprised. He didn't say anything for a little while. He looked as though he didn't know what to say. Then he said, "You don't have to plant another flower there. I have plenty of flowers. I'm just a selfish old man. I'm glad you're not selfish."

Well, Tommy got to be a good friend of the old neighbor. By and by Tommy told him his Sunday school lesson each week. He always ended by talking about Jesus — how Jesus loved him and was with him and helped him. Mr. Nelson often asked Tommy questions about Jesus.

241

One day Tommy was extra happy. Old Mr. Nelson promised to go to church with Tommy and his family. The next Sunday Mr. Nelson was all dressed up and waiting on the porch when Tommy got up. He had another happy surprise for Tommy, too. His housekeeper wanted to come along.

After going to Bible class and church for a while, Mr. Nelson and his housekeeper were sure that Jesus was their Savior. So they joined the pastor's class and became members of Tommy's church.

How did Tommy get to be a good salesman for Jesus? By being polite and friendly. He was willing to admit his mistakes and was humble, or "small." That's why God could make Tommy a big success in winning people for Him and for His church.

Questions to ask and answer: How did Tommy make himself small when the old man scolded him? What did Mr. Nelson say when he saw that Tommy was sorry and polite? How did Tommy become a big success in God's eyes? Why was the old man willing to listen to Tommy's talk about Jesus? Can you say the Bible words from memory?

Bible reading on how to become big: Matthew 23:1-12.

Let us bow and pray: Dear Father in heaven, please make us willing to be small so that You can make us big. Please make us a great success especially in leading others to You, through Jesus Christ, our Lord. Amen.

*We are God's work, made in Christ Jesus
for good works.* Ephesians 2:10

Made for Good Works

Mrs. Johnson broke her leg in falling down some steps. When she came home from the hospital, she just didn't know how she'd get along. She was a widow and lived all alone.

Before she could get her coat off, Mary Jane and Louise came over. They had seen her come in a taxi and decided to help her.

"What would you like for dinner?" Mary Jane asked. "I'm going to make it for you."

"Here, let me help you get that coat off so you can sit down," said Louise, bringing a chair.

"You shouldn't be doing this," said Mrs. Johnson, even though she felt real glad that the girls had come.

"Of course we should," said Louise. "That's what we were made for."

Mary Jane got the idea right away and agreed. "Sure," she said with a twinkle in her eye. "God made us His children so that we would help you when your leg was broken."

At first Mrs. Johnson thought the girls were joking. "Do you girls really believe that?" she asked.

"Yes, Mrs. Johnson," said Louise seriously. "God saved us and made us His children so that we will do good works. That's what the Bible says."

"I do declare," said Mrs. Johnson. "I always heard that Christians think they don't have to do good because they are saved by faith."

"Sure," Mary Jane explained. "The Bible says we are saved by grace, through faith in Jesus. But God makes us

His children so that we will do good works. And right now our best chance to do some good is right here, if you'll let us."

"I do declare," said Mrs. Johnson again as she sat down to watch the girls enjoy helping her.

Questions to think about: Why did the girls come over to Mrs. Johnson's house? What did they tell Mrs. Johnson? Why did she think the girls were joking? What wrong idea did Mrs. Johnson have about Christians? What does the Bible verse say is God's reason for making us His children?

Bible reading for older children and adults: Ephesians 2:4-10.

Our prayer: Dear Father in heaven, we are thankful that we have been made Your children through the love of Jesus. Please make us also the most useful people we can be. Give us the Holy Spirit so that we will gladly do good in whatever ways we can. In Jesus' name we ask it. Amen.

Do not worry, saying, "What shall we eat?" or "What shall we drink?" or "What shall we wear?" Matthew 6:31

How to Worry Less

Jack and his dad were looking at some wall cards in a drugstore. The cards were little signs with sayings on them.

"Look at this one, Jack," said his dad. "I think I'll buy it for our home. It may help us."

Jack looked at the card. It said, "Why worry when you can pray?"

244

"Yes, sir," said his father. "If we'd pray more, we wouldn't worry quite so much, that's for sure."

When they came home with the card, Jack's mother said, "I'm sure I need that little reminder. Whenever we get company, I worry about what to serve them. I worry about our bills and about my children and about getting my work done. Guess I'll have to pray more."

As they were talking, Ruth came into the room. She was going to a young people's party at the church. "Mother," she said, "there's a spot in my dress, and I can't wear it. What'll I wear? I haven't a thing to wear. It's awful."

Then Jack showed Ruth the little sign which said, "Why worry when you can pray?" At first it made Ruth angry. Then she laughed and said, "If I'd talk to God about my dress, I'm sure it wouldn't seem to matter much. I do have other dresses."

And so that family learned the secret of how to worry less.

Jesus said, "Do not worry, saying, 'What shall we eat?' or 'What shall we drink?' or 'What shall we wear?'" People who keep Him in their hearts find that there's not much to worry about. They always have enough food and clothing or anything else they really need.

Questions to think about: What was on the card that Jacks father bought? What does the saying mean? Why did Jack's father buy the card? What did Jack's mother often worry about? What was Ruth worrying about? How did the card help her? Who can repeat what Jesus said about worrying?

Bible reading: Matthew 6:31-34.

Our prayer: Dear Father in heaven, we thank You for promising to take care of Your children. Help us to trust You for all the things we really need so that we will pray to You instead of worrying. In Jesus' name we ask it. Amen.

245

The whole earth is full
of God's glory. Isaiah 6:3

A World Full of God's Wonders

The boys were lying on the floor, looking at a new book their mother had just bought for them.

"Look, Mother," said Harry. "We don't see with our eyes in the front of our head. We see in the back with the brain!"

"And do you know something else about our eyes?" said his brother Paul. "There are lots of tiny wires going from the eye to the brain. That's how we see."

"Not real wires," said Harry, who had read a lot about people's bodies. "They're called nerves. Nerves are muscle wires."

"Only God could have made our wonderful bodies," said their mother "Our eyes and the way they work are a miracle."

Then the boys turned to a different page in the book and read some more. "Do you know how strong atoms are?" Paul asked. He could hardly believe what he was reading.

"Atoms are real tiny. There are a million atoms in one peanut. But the atoms in one peanut could push a train from New York to Los Angeles. It says so right here."

"Don't forget that God put this power into the atom," their mother reminded them. "He put it there when He made the earth and all that is in it. How great God is and how wonderful His works are!"

When the prophet Isaiah got some idea of how great God is, he heard the angels of God saying to one another: "Holy, holy, holy is the Lord of hosts. The whole earth is full of His glory." God's greatness and glory can be seen in everything He made.

But even more wonderful is what He did for us when He sent His Son Jesus to save us from our sins. God became a baby. Jesus was God living on earth as a man. This Jesus has "all power in heaven and on earth." He has the power "to save all who draw near to God through Him." That's how great God is!

Questions: What did the boys find out about their eyes? Why did their mother call this a miracle? How strong is an atom? Who gave the atom its power? What did Isaiah hear the angels say to one another? What is even more wonderful than the world God has made?

Bible reading for older children and adults: Isaiah 6:1-7.

We bow and pray: Dear Lord, we thank and praise You for the way You made us and the whole earth. But we love You most because You loved us even though we were sinful, and sent Your Son Jesus to die for us. We praise and thank You, O Lord, especially for that. Amen.

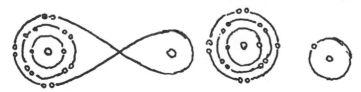

I will trust and will not
  be afraid. Isaiah 12:2

Because God Is Near

Billy was afraid to be alone in his upstairs bedroom without a light. So his mother tied a string to the pull switch and hung the string over the front bedpost. Now Billy could pull the string and turn the light on or off.

Then his mother sat down to talk to Billy. "Once there was a little boy lost in a woods. When night came and it was dark, he started to cry," she said. "Then something rubbed against his leg. It was his little dog. The boy was so glad to have his dog with him that he quit crying. A little later his father found him, and then the boy wasn't one bit afraid any more."

"I'm not afraid when Daddy is with me," said Billy.

"God is our Father in heaven," said his mother, "and He's always near us. And so is His Son Jesus. People who know that Jesus loves them say, 'I will trust and will not be afraid.'"

"I know Jesus loves me," said Billy. "But how can I learn to *trust* him?" asked Billy.

"Why do you trust *me?*" asked his mother.

"Because you come when I call."

"Well," said his mother, "Jesus is always closer to you than I can be. He said, 'I am with you always.' He loves you, and He can do much more for you than I can."

Billy thought about this for a few moments. Then he said, "Mother, I'll turn the light off when you go." When his mother left Billy said to Jesus, "I will trust and will not be afraid." Then he pulled the string, and soon he was fast asleep.

Questions to talk about: What story did Billy's mother tell him? Why? What made the little lost boy feel safe? Why did Billy trust his mother? Why can we trust God? Who can say the Bible words? What made Billy willing to go to sleep without a light?

Bible reading: Isaiah 12:1-6.

Our prayer: Dear loving Father in heaven, please forgive us for not always trusting You. Make us brave and happy. Remind us that Jesus, our Savior, is always near us and loves us. In Jesus' name we ask it. Amen.

First they gave themselves to the Lord. 2 Corinthians 8:5

What Jesus Wants from Us

A little girl had some very rich parents, but she seldom saw them. You see, while they traveled all over the world, she had to stay at home with a nurse.

One day the mother sent her little girl a beautiful and expensive doll. At first the girl didn't even want to open the package. When she saw the present, she threw the doll on the floor and broke it. Now, why do you suppose she did that?

Sobbing and crying, she said, "Oh, Mother, don't just send me pretty *things*. I want *you!*" She cried a long time.

Jesus isn't satisfied either when people give Him only things. Some people think He is pleased when they give His church a present now and then or when they give one of His children a gift. But He wants us — our hearts, our love, ourselves.

The first Christians were very good to others who needed help, though they themselves were poor. Can you guess why? The Bible says, "First they gave themselves to the Lord."

How can we give ourselves to the Lord? By believing that He is our Lord and Savior, by trusting in His promises, by being thankful, by letting Him rule us and own us, by living with Him and for Him, and by listening to what He tells us in His Word.

Have we given ourselves to Jesus? Let's remember that He wants *us*, not just some presents. He even died on a cross so that He could have us.

Questions to help us think: What made the little girl think that her parents didn't love her? Why did she break the present her mother sent her? Why isn't Jesus satisfied when people give Him only things? What does the Bible say the first Christians gave to the Lord? How can we give ourselves to Jesus?

Bible reading: 2 Corinthians 8:1-5.

Our prayer: Dear Lord, we love You, but our love sometimes gets very small and cold. Please keep us from ever giving You anything without also giving You our heart. Amen.

*Whatever you would want others to do to you,
do that to them.* Matthew 7:12

A Voice That Comes Back

A city boy named Billy went with his parents to visit some relatives on a farm. The next morning Billy got up early and took a walk by himself. It felt good to be out in the fresh air and in the open spaces.

Out in a field Billy began running like a horse. When he came to a woods, he stopped and shouted "Whoa!" to himself. Back came a voice that said "Whoa!" It sounded almost like Billy's.

Billy was surprised at this. He thought a boy was hiding among the trees. "Shut up!" yelled Billy. "Shut up!" the voice repeated. This made Billy angry. "I'll punch you in the nose!" he yelled. "I'll punch you in the nose!" said the voice.

Billy ran back to the house to tell his parents. "Mother," he said, "there's a mean boy in that woods. Whatever I say he says. When I told him to shut up, he yelled, 'Shut up!'"

His mother laughed. "Son," she said, "that voice was your echo. It said only what you said. If you had called

251

kind words into the woods, the voice would have answered you in a kind way."

"I hope you'll learn a lesson from this," said Billy's father, who had been listening. "Other people usually treat us the way we treat them. And Jesus gave us the Golden Rule, which tells us the way God wants us to treat other people. Do you remember it?"

"Yes," said Billy. "Whatever you would want others to do to you, do that to them."

"That's right," said his father. "When we follow this rule, we love our neighbor the way we would like to be loved. Then that love usually comes back to us."

"Of course, we all need a lot of help and practice in following the Golden Rule," said Billy's mother. "But Jesus makes us willing and able. His voice in us is a loving voice. Why don't you go back to the woods and try the echo once more?"

So, just for fun, Billy ran back to the woods and yelled, "Let's be friends." At once the echo shouted back, "Let's be friends."

Questions to talk about: What did Billy hear when he yelled "Whoa!" near a woods one morning? What did he think the echo was? What lesson did Billy's father want him to learn? Can you say the Golden Rule in your own words? Who makes us willing and able to follow this rule? What good reasons do we have for practicing this rule?

Bible reading: Luke 6:27-31.

Our prayer: Dear Lord Jesus, we are sorry that we don't always love others the way we want to be loved. Please forgive us, and help us to do to others what we would want others to do to us. Help us to make our echo sound like You so that Your love will speak through us and will come back to us also in what we say and do. Amen.

You may not take the name of the Lord,
your God, in vain. Exodus 20:7

What Can You Do?

A small boy often came down to his father's store on days when he didn't have school. His father had told him that someday the store would be his, so he wanted to learn the business.

One day one of the workers said to him, "You'll never amount to much — you're too small."

The boy answered, "I can do something you can't do."

"Oh?" said the man. "What?"

"I don't think I should tell you," said the boy.

But the man became curious and begged him to tell. So at last the boy said, "Well, I can keep from swearing, and you can't."

The man was very much ashamed, because he often said God's name without a good reason, and he knew this was wrong. But, like a lot of other people, he had gotten into the habit of cursing and swearing and no longer noticed it himself.

God's Law says: "You may not take the name of the Lord, your God, in vain." We should love God so much that we will not curse or swear or use God's name without a good reason.

In the Bible the apostle Paul said: "Whatever you do in word or deed, do all to the glory of God." Cursing and swearing dishonors God and never adds to His glory.

Instead of using God's name in vain, we ought to use His name in praying to Him, telling others about Him, and giving thanks to Him. Because we don't do this nearly enough, we are glad that God loves us and forgives us for Jesus' sake.

Questions to talk about: What could the boy do that a worker in his father's store couldn't do? How did the worker feel when the boy told him this? What do you think made him feel that way? Which commandment forbids us to use God's name without a good reason? What are some good ways of using God's name?

Bible reading: Philippians 2:5-13.

Our prayer: Dear Lord God, please forgive us the times we have used Your name in vain by saying it without talking to You or thinking about You. Keep us from using Your holy name for cursing and dirty talk or for no good reason at all. Help us to keep Your name holy and to use it in prayer and in praising You. We ask this in the name of Jesus, our Savior. Amen.

Let love be real. Romans 12:9

How Real Love Shows Itself

When Judy was sick, her brother Kenneth did her many favors. But when she was well again, he stopped being as kind as he had been.

"Kenneth, why can't you be as nice to Judy now as you were when she was sick?" his mother asked him one day. "I thought you told me you loved her."

"Sure I do," said Ken, "but Judy knows that without me being sweet to her all the time."

"But are you loving her when you aren't nice to her?" his mother asked. "Real love always shows itself. It's not enough just to *say* you love someone."

"You mean I can't love a person without doing something for him?" Ken asked.

254

"Not without *wanting* to do something for the person you love," his mother told him. "Tell me, did Jesus show His love for people?"

"Well, yes, He did," Ken admitted.

"Believe me," said his mother, "if your love is real, it will show. It will show itself in what you do."

"Okay," said Ken, and right then and there he decided he would try to love people by what he said and did. So he started saying "please" and "thank you" politely and tried to be more friendly and unselfish to Judy and to other people.

One day Judy told him, "You're the nicest brother I could have."

"And our home is so much happier since you decided to show your love," said his mother.

The Bible says, "Let love be real." It isn't real unless it is willing to act. Real love shows itself in loving behavior, just as Jesus showed His love in what He did.

Questions to help us think: When was Ken kind to Judy? What wrong idea did Ken have when Judy was well again? What did Ken's mother tell him? How did Jesus show His love for us? What kind of love does God want us to show?

Bible reading about love: John 15:12-17.

Our prayer: Dear heavenly Father, please help us to have a true love for other people, especially for those in our home. Forgive us the many times we have not shown love to others. Help us to remember that real love shows itself in loving words and deeds. Give us the Holy Spirit so that we will show love in whatever we do, through Jesus, who loved us and gave Himself for us. Amen.

*Let the beauty of the Lord, our God,
be on us.* Psalm 90:17

The Beauty That Comes from God

Once there was a little girl who wanted to be beautiful. "I wish I were pretty," she often said to herself. "Then people would love me more." So she combed and combed and combed her hair and wore pretty clothes and tried to smile and hold her head like a queen.

On a vacation in New Orleans the girl and her parents visited the streets where artists paint outside. "Please let the man paint a picture of me," the little girl begged. She thought the painter would make her look prettier than she was.

Her father agreed, so while the man painted her picture the little girl sat as straight and still as she could. "Please make it as pretty as you can," she said. "If it isn't pretty, I don't want it." The painter smiled and told her she would be as pretty as a picture.

The painter made the little girl look very pretty, because he wanted her to be pleased with his painting. But when he was finished, the father said, "I don't want that picture. It doesn't look like my girl at all. You've made her too pretty."

256

The little girl began to cry. She wanted so much to be like the girl in the picture. Then the father took her into his arms and said, "Sweetheart, you don't have to pretend to be prettier than you are. You are the dearest girl in the world to me, so why should I want a picture that doesn't look like you?"

When the little girl heard that her father loved her because she belonged to him, his love seemed much more important than looking pretty. This made the little girl happy, and right then and there she also became more beautiful.

God, our Father in heaven, loves us. He loves us so much that He let His Son Jesus die for us on a cross. He wants us to be His children. He doesn't care how we look on the outside, and He's willing to overlook our faults. All that He wants is our love. When we love Him, His love makes us beautiful. That's why the psalm writer said, "Let the beauty of the Lord, our God, be on us."

Let's talk about this: What was the little girl worrying about? Why did she want her picture painted? Why didn't her father like the painting? What did he tell her when she started to cry? How did his love make her feel? In what way is God like the little girl's father? Who can say what the psalm writer wrote?

Bible reading: Psalm 90:14-17.

Our prayer: Dear Father in heaven, help us to remember that it is much more important to be pretty on the inside than on the outside. Make us beautiful by filling our hearts with Your love, through Jesus Christ, our Lord. Amen.

We have gifts that differ according to the grace given to us. Romans 12:6

Different Kinds of Gifts

"Martha knows hardly anything in school," said Kay one evening. "She's so dumb."

"She held the organist's baby in church last Sunday," her mother answered. "I noticed some other girls sitting there who didn't help."

"You mean me, don't you, Mom," said Kay, blushing a little. "I was talking about *knowing* things."

"Knowing how to help someone and how to make a baby happy is knowing quite a bit," her mother explained. "You see, God has made every person different. We all have gifts from God that differ according to what He has given us. That's what the Bible tells us. We can't all be good in knowing lessons and books."

"Like our coach," said Fred. "He knows how to make boys quit fighting and be real friends."

"That's knowing how to be a peacemaker," said his dad. "And Ken, who tries hard in arithmetic but just can't catch on, is the best lifeguard I know."

"That's right," said Fred.

"So you see, Kay," her mother repeated, "just knowing things out of books isn't the only kind of knowing. Maybe we should learn this verse from the Bible to help us remember what we've talked about: 'We have gifts that differ according to the grace given to us.' Grace is the love and blessing of God."

Then they all said the verse together, and Kay decided she had learned a good lesson.

258

Questions to talk about: What didn't Martha know very well? At what was she very good? In what are some people that you know extra good? Why would a Christian father rather have friendly children with poor grades than unkind children with good grades? What does the Bible verse say we all have from God? What does God want us to do with whatever gifts He gives us?

Bible reading for older children and adults: Romans 12:3-10.

Let us pray: Thank You, dear Lord, for the gifts You have given us. Please keep us from ever being proud of what You give us. Help us to remember that different people have different gifts from You. Give us the Holy Spirit so that we will use our gifts in serving You and other people as well as we can. We ask this in Jesus' name. Amen.

I have you in my heart. Philippians 1:7

Pittakos Was Wrong

"You mark my words," said Pittakos, the pottery maker in Philippi, "that fellow Paul is planning to cheat somebody. He wouldn't preach and go around doing good things just for nothing. Nobody does."

"You could be wrong," said Philip, the saddle maker next door. "This Paul says he does it for one who is called Jesus. He says that Jesus is God and that this Jesus went about doing good when He lived on earth. He says this Jesus wants His disciples to do only good to other people."

"Nobody loves anyone but himself," said Pittakos. "Even those who say they love God or their neighbor are trying to get something for themselves."

259

But Pittakos was wrong. Even though the first part of the story was made up, Paul did go to Philippi. There some people believed what He told them about Jesus. Others hated him and told lies about him. Some were sure his preaching was a trick to make money.

When Paul later wrote a letter to the Christians in Philippi, he told why he went to so much trouble to bring the Gospel to them. "I have you in my heart," he wrote. This meant, "I love you." He said he wanted them to get the blessings of Jesus and to grow up to be good people.

Every pastor who loves Jesus feels as Paul did. He is willing to do extra-hard and -good things for people. He works to lead them to love Jesus and to help them become the kind of people God wants them to be. Our pastor also says to us, "I have you in my heart."

Fathers and mothers do much for their children because they have them in their hearts. And parents who love Jesus want their children to have His love so that they will become more and more like Him.

Do you have anyone in your heart? See if you can think of someone who doesn't know Jesus, and talk over ways of showing him the love of our Lord. If he wants to know why you are being good to him, say, "I have you in my heart."

Let's talk about this: What did some folks think was Paul's reason for preaching in their town? What did Paul say was his reason? Who are some of the people teaching us the Word of God? What do you think is their reason for doing it? How can we be a little bit like Paul?

Bible reading for older children and grownups: Philippians 1:3-11.

Let us pray: Dear God, we thank You for people like Paul, who spread the Good News about Jesus. Please open our hearts to others, that we may love them and help them to grow in Jesus' love. In His name we ask it. Amen.

The Lord is my Shepherd. Psalm 23:1

When the Good Shepherd Calls

In the beautiful country of Scotland there was a shepherd who had a little daughter. Often he would take her with him when he led his sheep to green pastures or to pools of fresh water in the valleys.

The little girl loved to be with her father and his sheep. Most of all she liked to hear him call his sheep and see the sheep come to him when he called.

When the girl became a young woman, she went away to work in a big city. At first she wrote to her father every week, but soon the time between letters became longer and longer. At last she stopped writing altogether.

One day a young man from her village saw her in the big city and spoke to her. But she acted as though she had never seen him before. Later some other people told him that she often got drunk and lived with men who weren't married to her.

When the young man returned home, he told the shepherd what he had heard about the daughter. At once the shepherd started out to look for her. Day after day he walked up and down the streets of the big city, hoping to find her.

Then he remembered how his little girl used to listen to him call his sheep. So he went through the streets of the city again, this time giving his shepherd's call.

When the daughter heard her father's voice, she knew at once who it was. Quickly she ran out to the street to find him. He took her into his arms and asked her to go back home with him. Because she saw how much he loved her, she went back with him and became a decent, lovely woman again.

Jesus said, "I am the Good Shepherd." We are His sheep. He even gave His life to save His sheep. His sheep know His voice. It is a loving, forgiving, inviting voice, which His sheep love to hear and gladly follow.

"The Lord is my Shepherd," we say in Psalm 23. He calls us away from our sins and leads us back to a beautiful life with God. His love makes us glad to go with Him and makes us want to be decent for His sake.

Questions to talk about: What did the young woman enjoy hearing when she was a little girl? What happened when she left her father and went to a big city by herself? How did her father find her? Why did she go back home with him? Who is our Shepherd? Why is He called the Good Shepherd?

Bible reading to say together: Psalm 23.

Let us pray: Dear Jesus, we're glad that You love us and that You are our Good Shepherd. Whenever we leave You by doing wrong or forgetting You, please call us by Your love to follow You to Your heavenly home. Amen.

Why not rather suffer wrong? Why not rather
let yourselves be cheated? 1 Corinthians 6:7

When It's Better to Lose

Jim and Gene were quarreling at the breakfast table. Over what? Over a little cardboard picture from a cereal box.

"Give it to me," said Jim. "It's mine. You got the last one."

"I saw it first," said Gene, "and I'm keeping it."

"Why quarrel over a piece of paper?" their older sister asked them. "Is it worth a quarrel?"

"Well, Gene shouldn't be selfish," said Jim.

"Yeah, and you shouldn't be selfish either," said Gene, and they just about started the fight all over again.

So their mother sat down to talk to them. "Boys," she said, "once many of the Christians in Corinth were quarreling. They were saying nasty things about each other. They even went to the heathen judges and asked them to punish the Christians with whom they quarreled. Do you know what the apostle Paul told them?"

"He told them to quit fighting," Jim guessed.

"Yes, he did. He said, 'When you have a fight, you've already lost more than the fight.' Can you guess what that might be?"

Both boys thought a while, and their mother just sat and waited. "Well," said Gene, "it might be your temper and your happy feelings." "And you could lose your friends and your friendship with God," added Jim.

"Right," said their mother. "That's why St. Paul wrote, 'Isn't it better to let someone be unkind to you? Isn't it better to let yourself be cheated?' So what do you think he'd say to you, Jim?"

"Well," said Jim, a little ashamed. "I suppose he'd say, 'Jim, why don't you let Gene have that old card? You'll lose something more important by fighting.'"

"Now you're thinking," said his mother. "And you may lose your selfishness if you'd rather let yourself be cheated than to fight and cheat. I'm sure God would prefer that. What do you think?"

Without doing any more thinking, Gene handed the card to his brother and said, "Here's your card, Jim. I'm sorry I was selfish." In doing that, Gene lost his bad feelings, which is something everybody wants to lose.

Questions to talk about: What were Jim and Gene quarreling about? Why wasn't the card worth a fight? What makes people quarrel over almost nothing? What did the apostle Paul tell some quarreling Christians in the Bible? What may a Christian lose if he fights?

Bible reading about cheating and other sins: 1 Corinthians 6:7-11.

Our prayer: Dear heavenly Father, please forgive all the quarrels and the mean words that have come from our selfish hearts. Give us the Spirit of Jesus, our Lord, so that we will *take* wrong rather than *do* wrong, and *be* cheated rather than *cheat* or lose our Christian spirit. Help us to become what You want us to be, for the sake of Jesus, who died to save us. Amen.

You ask and do not receive,
because you ask wrongly. James 4:3

When God Says "No"

Once an old Christian grandfather was asked by some people to pray to God for rain. They knew he prayed a lot. Before he prayed, he decided to find out what day would be best for rain.

Well, many of the women didn't want it to rain on Monday, because that was their washday. On Tuesday the people who went to the lakes and those who had planned a picnic wanted clear weather. On Wednesday the farmers were going to cut their hay, and on Thursday they wanted the hay to dry. On Friday there was a ball game, and on Saturday many city people wanted to work in their yards and gardens. On Sunday, of course, the ministers didn't want rain to keep people from coming to church.

There was no day that suited everyone, so the old grandfather asked the Lord to send the rain whenever He thought it best, and that's the way He sends it.

This is just a story, but what it teaches is true. Sometimes we pray for good weather because we have something planned. When we wake up the next morning and it's raining, we may think that God didn't hear our prayer or doesn't care about us.

265

But God cares about all His people, and He does what is best for all. That's why He seldom answers a selfish prayer. A selfish prayer asks for things that may harm other people.

Think of what would happen if every day one person would ask God to keep the rain from falling, and if God always did what was asked. There would soon be nothing to eat, because food cannot grow without rain.

The Bible says to people who pray selfish prayers, "You ask and do not receive, because you ask wrongly." Jesus prayed to His heavenly Father, "Not My will, but Yours, be done." From Jesus we learn to let God decide what is best for all when we pray. Then our prayers are always answered.

Questions to help us think: What did the grandfather try to find out when he was asked to pray for rain? What did he find out? What did he finally ask the Lord to do? Why doesn't God answer selfish prayers? How did Jesus pray in the Garden before dying to save us from our sins? What can we learn from this prayer?

Bible reading: Matthew 26:36-44.

Our prayer:

> Dear Father, change my will today;
> Make it like Yours and take away
> All that now makes it hard to say,
> "Your will be done." Amen.

I know whom I have believed. 2 Timothy 1:12

It's Not What You Know

"Gordon is real smart," said Jack. "He's learning 600 Bible verses and where they are in the Bible. Next year I'm going to try to do that."

"He knows just about all of them," said Ann. "He said 50 last Sunday. It took almost the whole Sunday school hour to say them."

Jack began to be a little jealous. "Mrs. Rogers was real proud of Gordon, but you know what he did? He stole some money from the offering once," said Jack.

"I wish you hadn't mentioned that," his dad told him. "Gordon said he was sorry, and he promised not to do it again. So, Jack, let's not tell anybody, not anybody, ever again."

"I'm sorry," said Jack, and he meant it because he knew he had done wrong.

"Could you know 600 Bible verses and not be a Christian?" asked Ann.

"How many verses do you think the devil knows?" asked her father.

"Oh, he probably knows them all," said Ann.

"So you see, just knowing Bible verses doesn't make anyone a Christian," said her dad. "It's not *what* you know but *whom* you know that counts."

"That's right," said Ann's mother, who had been listening. "St. Paul told his friend Timothy, 'I know *whom* I have believed.' He didn't say, 'I know *what* I have believed.' He knew Jesus and believed Him. That's why he was such a good Christian."

Of course, knowing Bible verses is also good if we let God talk to us through these words. And knowing Bible stories is very good, too, because they tell us about God's ways and God's people. But knowing that Jesus is our Lord and Savior, and being one of His close friends, is best of all. That's what makes a person a Christian.

Questions to talk about: What was Gordon learning? Why can a person know many Bible verses and still not be a Christian? What good is it to know Bible verses and Bible stories? What is most important of all? Why is knowing Jesus most important?

Bible reading for older children and adults: 2 Timothy 1:8-12.

Let us pray: Lord Jesus, we are glad that we know You and that You love us and are our Savior. Please keep us close to You in Your kingdom until we are with You forever in heaven. Amen.

In Jesus we have . . . the forgiveness of sins. Colossians 1:14

The Best Thing in the World

"Daddy, what is the worst thing in the world?" little Amy asked one evening at the supper table.

"What do you think?" he asked.

"I think the worst thing in the world is being sick a long time and not being able to play outside," she said.

Her father answered, "Good health is a great blessing, but some of the best and happiest people in the world are sick people. God often blesses His children through their sickness."

"I think the worst thing in the world is to be poor," said Amy's brother Glen. "Could you raise my allowance, Dad?" he asked with a grin.

"God feels sorry for the poor, and He wants us to help them, but He has promised that His children will always have what they need. And He warns us against loving money. Maybe I should cut your allowance," Glen's father said, grinning also.

"I think being stupid is the worst trouble a person could have," said James, who was going to college. "People who don't learn much and can't think straight aren't able to take care of themselves."

His father agreed and said, "A good mind and a good education are important blessings, but there are many happy and good people who have had very little education. And many rascals have gone to college," he added.

"I know the worst thing in the world," said Amy, who had been thinking. "*Sin* is the worst thing in the world. Pastor Jacobs said it's to blame for all other troubles."

"You're right," said her father. "Before Adam and Eve sinned, they had no sickness and no trouble. Best of all, they weren't in any trouble with God, so they were always happy. If sin is the *worst trouble,* what is the *best blessing* in the world?"

"I know that, too," said Amy. "The forgiveness of sins."

"I'm sure that's right," her father agreed. "Nothing is more important than having God's forgiveness and His love all the time. And we can have it all the time by trusting in Jesus to save us. As the Bible tells us, 'In Jesus we have . . . the forgiveness of sins.'"

Let's talk about this: What was Amy's question? At first, what did she think the worst thing might be? Why is sin the worst trouble in the world? What is God's best blessing? How can we have forgiveness all the time? Let's say the Bible words together.

Bible reading: Psalm 130.

Let us pray: Dear Father in heaven, we thank and praise You for sending Jesus to save us. Help us to believe that "in Him we have the forgiveness of sins" so that we will also have the joy of salvation, through Jesus Christ, our Lord. Amen.

Where sin was great, God's love was even greater. Romans 5:20

Always More Love than We Need

It was bedtime, and Mrs. Martin was up in her daughter Ann's room for a good-night talk and for prayer.

"Mother," said Ann, "I don't think I can ever be good." She was crying, because she had been scolded quite a bit that day.

"You're a good girl now," said her mother, "because you're sorry about what you've done wrong."

"But I mean *really* good, the way God wants me to be," said Ann.

"Do you think *I'm* that good?" her mother asked.

"Well, maybe" the girl said, hating to say No. "But I love you anyway because you're good to me."

270

"Do you think your daddy is as good as God wants us to be?" her mother asked.

"Yes," said Ann. "Daddy never does anything wrong."

"You ask him," said her mother. "He'll tell you that he does wrong things, too, even though he doesn't want to. Is our pastor as good as God wants him to be?"

This time Ann was very sure. "He must be, or he couldn't be a pastor," she answered.

"But he said last Sunday that he wasn't," Ann's mother reminded her. "Nobody is as good as God wants him to be. The Bible says there is not a person on earth who does only good and never sins."

"But I do so many wrong things," said Ann.

"I'm glad you care," said her mother. "I do many wrong things, too. But God loves us just the same, and that's why we love Him. The Bible says, 'Where sin abounded, grace did much more abound.'"

"What does that mean?" asked Ann.

"Let's learn it this way," said her mother: "'Where sin was great, God's love was much, much greater.' You see, God's love is greater than any sin, and greater than all our sins put together."

"Does that mean God is always willing to forgive us, no matter how much we do wrong?" asked Ann.

"Yes," said her mother, "that's what's so wonderful about God's love. We're always forgiven because Jesus paid for all sins. God's love doesn't depend on how good we are. It just depends on whether we are sorry and really want His forgiveness."

Questions: What worried Ann? Who did Ann think was as good as God wants a person to be? What did Ann's mother tell her? Why does God love us even though we often sin? What does the Bible mean when it says, "Where sin was great, God's love was even greater"?

Bible reading for good readers: Romans 3:19-24.

Our prayer: Dear Father in heaven, we are glad that Your love is greater than all our sins. Please keep on giving us Your love, and make us what You want us to be, for Jesus' sake. Amen.

Hallowed be Thy name. Matthew 6:9

Honoring God's Holy Name

The Smith family was having devotions around the supper table. At the close they all prayed the Lord's Prayer. Little Karen prayed along, too. She was only three.

When they were finished, Mrs. Smith said, "Karen, tell me how you say the part after 'Our Father, who art in heaven.'"

Everybody listened. Karen couldn't say an "R." She said, "Owah Fathah, who awt in heaven, Hawold be Thy name."

"I thought that's what you said," her mother told her. "Look, Karen, not *Harold. Hallowed* be Thy name." Then she repeated it a few times until Karen said it right.

"What does hallowed mean?" asked Jack, who was seven.

"It means to make something seem holy and great. We pray that God's name will seem great and good to all people," said his mother, "because it is holy and great and good."

"God's name is kept holy when people learn the truth about God and also when Christians do what is right and good," his father added. "It's like the American soldier in Japan. When he got drunk and made trouble, people said, 'America is no good.'"

272

"Tell us in your own words, Daddy, what you think when you pray, 'Hallowed be Thy name,'" Mrs. Smith suggested.

"I might think of it this way," said Mr. Smith: "Our Father in heaven, may we do all things in such a way that people will have great respect for Your name and will admire and honor You. Keep me from ever disgracing Your name, and help me to show and teach other people Your love and goodness in sending Jesus to save me."

The last point is especially important. When people learn how wonderful Jesus is, then they begin to love our Father in heaven for sending His Son Jesus to save us. And when they love God, then they honor Him and His name.

Questions to help us think: What were the Smiths doing around the supper table? What mistake did Karen make in praying the Lord's Prayer? What does the word "hallowed" mean? Tell in your own words what you pray for when you say, "Hallowed be Thy name." When do people honor and worship God?

A psalm that honors God's name: Psalm 34:1-10.

Let us pray: Holy God, we praise Your name for all Your goodness toward us, especially for Your forgiveness of all our sins. Please give us the Holy Spirit so that we will honor You by being good Christians, through Jesus Christ, our Lord. Amen.

We should not depend on ourselves but on God. 2 Corinthians 1:9

Depending on God

It was a cold winter day. The sidewalk was slippery, and in places that weren't shoveled there was a lot of snow. Danny and his father were walking to the store together.

"I don't need you," said Danny when his father tried to hold his hand. "I can walk by myself." But pretty soon he fell down on the hard ice and started to cry.

"I'll take hold of your coat, Daddy," he said as they walked on. But in the deep snow he stumbled, and down he went again.

"Daddy, you take my hand," said Danny this time after he had stopped crying. So his daddy took his hand. When Dan slipped again, his daddy held him up and kept him from falling.

"It's better when you hold me than when I hold you," said Dan.

"Right," said his daddy. "And it's even better to let God hold us. That's what it means to trust in God. When we trust in God, we hold on to God, and then He holds us up and helps us."

274

Even the apostle Paul had to learn this lesson. He got into so much trouble that he thought he would soon be dead. Then he depended on God to help him, and God got him out of his trouble.

Sometimes God lets trouble happen to show us that we don't have a good strong hold on Him. When we ask God to take hold of us, things go better. That's how we learn that "we should not depend on ourselves but on God." We can depend on God because He loves us for Jesus' sake.

Questions to think about: Why did little Danny keep on falling down? When didn't he fall any more? How did the apostle Paul learn to trust God? What does our Bible verse tell us? Why can we trust God and depend on Him?

Bible reading: Psalm 25:1-7.

Let us pray: Dear Lord, take my hand and lead me every day. I trust in Your love and power, O Lord. Please keep me from falling into sins and other great troubles, and pick me up when I do fall, for Jesus' sake. Amen.

*The Lord is right in all His ways
and kind in all His doings.* Psalm 145:17

Always Right and Kind

"Mr. Alton died last night," Flora's mother reported at the supper table.

"You mean Jack's daddy?" asked Flora. "I saw him yesterday. He was working in the yard. What happened? Why did he have to die? He wasn't old and sick."

"Many people die before they get old," her mother answered. "God decides how long each one of us may live

275

here on earth. And God is right and good in everything He does."

"Didn't God want Mr. Alton to take care of Jack any longer? Who will take care of Jack and his mother? Will she have to get a job?" Flora asked. "Why did God let him die?"

"Now just a minute," her father said. "Aren't you forgetting what your mother told you? The Bible says, 'The Lord is right in all His ways and kind in all His doings.' We don't always know God's special reasons, but God must have had a *good* reason for letting Mr. Alton die. Maybe he was saved from much suffering."

"Maybe he was also kept from losing his faith in Jesus," said Flora's older brother Bob.

"That would be the best reason God could have for letting someone die," said his father. "People who believe in Jesus never *really* die. They go on living with God in heaven, where nobody ever dies."

"But what will happen to Jack and his mother?" Flora asked again.

"I'm glad you care," said her mother. "Let's try to find out if we can help them. In the meantime why don't we ask *God* to help them, too. I'm sure He will."

So they prayed, and the next morning Flora's mother went with Flora to see what they could do for Jack and his mother.

Questions to talk about: Who decides how long a person may live on earth? What may be some of God's reasons for letting people die before they are old? What does the Bible say about everything God does? Where did Jack's father go when he died if he belonged to Jesus? Why is that better than living on earth? Who can always take care of the people who need help on earth?

Bible reading for older children and grownups: John 11: 20-27.

Our prayer: Dear God, our Father in heaven, help us to believe that You are right and good in all that You do. Also when the sadness of death comes, help us to think of the blessings that come to Your children through Jesus Christ, our Lord. Give us the Holy Spirit so that we will always trust in Your love, no matter what happens. Amen.

The love of money is the root of all evils. 1 Timothy 6:10

The Love of Money

Bonnie heard about a family which used stories from the newspapers for family devotions. So Bonnie's dad took a big old picture frame and put some cork board into it. Then he told everybody to look for stories to talk about on Friday, and to tack them up on the board.

The very first week there was a story about a man who killed two people when he robbed a bank. Another story told about two young boys who knocked down an old lady and took her purse. And the church paper reported that someone broke into the Sunday school office and took the mission offering box.

"They all wanted money," said Bonnie when they talked about the stories around the supper table.

"And they all hurt other people to get it," said Fred.

"Why is it always money that makes people do wrong?" asked Bonnie.

"Not quite always," said her mother.

"But look," said Fred, "a man kills two people to get money. Two boys hurt a lady to get her purse. And some kids take the money that was supposed to help our missionaries. Always somebody gets hurt because people love money."

"Don't forget they also hurt themselves and God," said their dad. "Jesus had to suffer and die for the sins of stealing and coveting. His friend Judas even betrayed him for 30 pieces of silver. It's just as the Bible says, 'The love of money is the root of all evils.'"

"Is it better to be poor than rich?" asked Fred, a little worried because his father had a good business.

"That depends," said his father. "It's not the money but the *love* of money that causes the trouble. I hope you'll grow up without loving it. When you love God, He gives you what you need when you need it, and enough to help other people, too."

Questions: What kind of devotions did Bonnie's family have on Fridays? What was put on the board during the first week? What did all these people try to get? What does the Bible say about the love of money?

Bible reading for good readers: 1 Timothy 6:6-11.

Our prayer: Thank You, dear Father in heaven, for giving us money to buy the things we need and to do the good You want us to do. Please keep us from ever loving money and doing wrong to get it. Help us to remember that if we have Your love, You will give us what You want us to have. In Jesus' name we ask this. Amen.

As many as are led by the Spirit of God,
they are the children of God. Romans 8:14

Am I a Child of God?

"Mother," said Jack, who wanted very much to be a good Christian, "I do so many things that are wrong. Are you sure I'm one of God's children?"

"Well, now," she said, "that's an important question, and we need to be sure of the answer. The Bible says, 'Whoever has been baptized into Christ has put on Christ.' Have you been baptized?"

"Yes," said Jack.

"And do you believe that Jesus is your Savior and that He washes away your sins with His love?"

"Yes," said Jack.

"Well, then you're a Christian. The Bible says, 'You are all the children of God by trusting in Christ Jesus.'"

"But I do so many things that are wrong," said Jack.

"We all do things that are wrong," said his mother. "That's because we're sinners. If we had to be perfect in everything we do, no one could be a child of God."

"But don't we have to be perfect to be in heaven?" asked Jack.

"Yes," his mother told him, "but we are perfect in God's eyes only when Jesus covers up our sins. He does this when we ask Him to be our Savior."

"You know something else?" Jack's mother added. "When we believe in Jesus, He also gives us the Holy Spirit. That's why the Bible says, 'As many as are led by the Spirit of God, they are the children of God.'"

279

Questions to help us think: What worried Jack? What makes us God's children? How do Christians become perfect? How do people receive the Holy Spirit? Why will the Spirit of God always lead us to do what is right and good? Who can say the Bible verse from memory?

Bible reading for older children and adults: Romans 8:9-14.

Our prayer: We thank You, Holy Spirit, for leading us to love Jesus and to be sorry for our sins. Help us to please Him in all things so that we will be good children of our Father in heaven. We ask this in Jesus' name. Amen.

Love covers many sins. 1 Peter 4:8

Why Paul Helped His Sister

"Oh, oh, now there's a big spot on the clean tablecloth," said Paul to his sister Ruth. Ruth was setting the table to help her mother, who was at the store. Ruth wasn't supposed to open the new catsup bottle, but she did, and the catsup "popped" out.

"Please don't tell Mother," said Ruth. "I wanted this to be a nice surprise for her. I'll put on a clean tablecloth, and I'll wash the spot out later. I don't want Mother to think I don't mind her."

"Okay," said Paul. "Let's change it fast. I'll help you."

So they had the new cloth on the table before their mother came back, and everything looked lovely. "Honey, you're a good little housekeeper," she said, and kissed Ruth.

When they were alone, Ruth said to Paul, "Thanks for helping me out. I didn't mean to do wrong. I'm glad it wasn't noticed."

280

"At first I wasn't going to, but then I thought of a Bible verse," said Paul.

"Which verse?" asked Ruth.

"Love covers many sins," he told her. "That's the way we learned it in easy English."

"You did cover my sin," said Ruth. "It was Christian love."

"I wouldn't have if you had wanted to do something wrong. But I could see you were sorry," said Paul. "Why don't you tell Mom? She'll understand."

"Guess I will," said Ruth. "Then I'll feel better. And I'm sure she'll forgive me because she loves me."

Questions to talk about: What did Ruth do that was wrong? Why was she sorry? How did her brother help her? When might it be wrong to cover up a sin as Paul did? What is another way in which "love covers many sins"? Why are Christians willing to forgive other people?

Bible reading for older children and grownups: 1 Peter 4:7-10.

Our prayer: Dear Lord, we are happy because You forgive the clumsy and wrong things we do. Please make us willing to cover up the sins of others, and to help them straighten out what they do wrong. In Jesus' name we ask it. Amen.

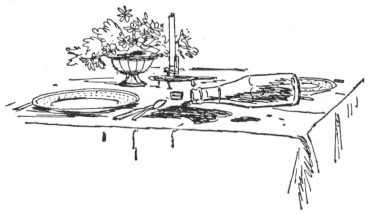

The disciples were filled with joy
and with the Holy Spirit. Acts 13:52

Glad to Have Trouble

Did you ever hear of anyone glad to have trouble? The believers in Antioch were. Almost their whole city came to hear Paul and Barnabas preach. But those who hated Jesus made trouble. Paul and Barnabas had to hurry away.

When this happened, did the Christians cry? No, they didn't. The Bible says, "They were filled with joy and with the Holy Spirit." They were glad they had found out that Jesus was their Savior, and they were willing to be hurt for loving Him.

What will make us glad to have trouble for Jesus? Our love. If we will love Him enough, we won't mind the trouble.

Grandma Jackson had to work hard to get a big dinner ready whenever her children and grandchildren came to visit. Did she mind? No. Why not? Because she loved them. Love made her glad to have trouble.

Mr. Decker gave up his fishing trip to get his boy from the hospital. Was he sorry to do it? No, he was glad he could. Why? Because he loved his boy. Love makes us glad to have trouble for the people we love.

The new believers in Antioch were glad to have trouble for Jesus because they loved Him. They had just heard how much He had done for them. So they were willing to have some trouble for Him, too. Instead of being sad or afraid, "they were filled with joy and with the Holy Spirit," says the Bible.

What will make us glad to take on some trouble for Jesus? When we remember how He suffered and died for
282

us and when we love Him as our Savior, then we don't mind any trouble we have because of Him. Instead, it makes us glad.

Let's think about this: Why were the believers in Antioch glad when they heard Paul and Barnabas preach? Who made trouble? Why didn't this stop the believers from being glad? What can make anybody glad to have trouble? What will make us glad to have some trouble for Jesus?

Bible reading: Acts 13:44-52.

Our prayer: Dear Lord, our God, please help us to understand how much Jesus did for us, so that we will be glad even to have trouble for His sake. Fill us with joy and with the Holy Spirit as You did the believers in Antioch long ago. We ask this in Jesus' name. Amen.

Let us not get tired of doing good. Galatians 6:9

Piano Practice Can Be Fun

"Guess what!" said Patty to her friend Jill. "I'm starting piano lessons tomorrow. I'm so glad!"

But three months later she said, "Mother, do I *have* to practice playing the piano? I'm tired of it."

"Honey," said her mother, "most things worth learning are hard to do at first. But you mustn't give up so easily. You'll never become a piano player that way."

"But it takes so long to learn," Patty complained.

"I know it," said her mother. "But keep it up, and pretty soon you'll like it real well. Then you'll be glad you didn't quit when it was hard."

A few weeks later, at the Sunday dinner table, Patty said, "Being a Christian is like playing the piano, isn't it?"

"In what way is piano playing like being a Christian?" her father asked.

"Well," said Patty, "today our pastor told us not to get tired of doing good. 'If you don't quit, someday you'll be glad you didn't,' he said. That's what Mother told me about piano practice."

"I'm sure we all get tired of doing good at times," said Pat's mother. "Yesterday I thought, 'Why do I have to have all the children in the block at my house?' It makes more work for me. I get tired of doing it."

"And I get tired of working at the church," Pat's father said. "But whenever I do it, I enjoy it, and the more I do for God, the more I enjoy it."

"See what I mean?" said Pat. "Being a Christian is like playing the piano. The more I practice and the better I play, the more I like it."

That's why the Bible says, "So, then, whenever we can, let us do good to all men, especially to those who are members of our family of faith."

Questions to help us think: What did Patty get tired of doing? What did her mother tell her? What did the pastor preach about? In what way is being a Christian like piano practice?

Bible reading: Galatians 6:7-10.

Our prayer: Lord Jesus, we are glad that You didn't get tired of saving and helping people. Please keep us from getting tired of doing good for You so that we will be a blessing to others as You are to us. Amen.

284

*Don't just decorate yourself on the outside,
but be pretty on the inside.* 1 Peter 3:3, 4

The Best Way to Be Pretty

Kay and Karen giggled as they came down the stairs. They were wearing some hats that their mother had worn a long time ago, and some silk dresses that were much too long, and some fancy shoes they could hardly keep on their feet.

They giggled still more when they heard their mother come to see what they were doing, and then they burst out laughing. Their mother laughed, too. "My, how pretty my little girls look today," she said.

"These were pretty clothes long ago, weren't they, Mother?" said Kay.

"They were my prettiest clothes," her mother told her. "They look funny now because nobody wears that kind any more. Clothes change. But I know a way of dressing up that never changes and never gets old."

"You do?" asked Karen. She wanted to know all about it.

"Yes," her mother explained, "by dressing up on the inside you will always be pretty."

"But how can we dress up on the inside?" asked Karen.

"Well, you see," said her mother, "you are more than just a body. You are also a person living inside your body. The Bible calls this inside person the heart or soul. This part of you, you can dress and decorate by being kind and friendly and sweet and cheerful."

"Jesus gives us those clothes, doesn't He, Mother?" said Kay, beginning to understand.

"That's right," said her mother. "And God wants everybody to be pretty on the inside. In the Bible Peter wrote, 'Don't just decorate yourself on the outside, but be pretty on the inside.'"

Kay looked at her shoes and dress. "Is it wrong to dress up and be pretty on the outside?" she asked.

"No," her mother answered, "it's not wrong, but it's not important. It's much more important to be pretty on the inside, because that's what God wants to see."

Let's talk about this: What were the girls giggling about? When were those old clothes pretty? Why doesn't that kind of "pretty" stay pretty? In what way does God want us to be pretty? Why is it better to be pretty on the inside? How can we become pretty on the inside?

Bible reading for older children and adults: 1 Peter 3:3, 4.

Let us ask God to make us prettier on the inside: Dear God, we're glad that You love us even when we aren't pretty. Please make us pretty on the inside by giving us Jesus' love and the Holy Spirit. Teach us to be kind, lovely, clean, and friendly inside, and forgive us when we are mean and selfish and proud. We ask this in the name of Jesus, our beautiful Savior. Amen.

*No one can snatch you out
of God's hand.* John 10:30

Because God Is Holding Us

The wind was blowing hard, and the boat was going from one side to the other. Little Carol was afraid. She held on to her mother tightly. Her father rowed toward the shore as fast as he could. They had been fishing out on the lake when the storm started.

"Mommie, I can't hold on any tighter. Don't let me fall out of the boat," cried Carol.

Her mother said, "Don't worry, Carol. Mommie is holding you."

Carol was holding on to her mother, but her mother was also holding Carol. And her mother's arms were much stronger than Carol's. So Carol was safe because her mother held her close to her.

Some people are afraid they will not be able to hold on to Jesus. Jimmy was afraid. He said, "I told three lies last week, and I quarreled with my sister. Maybe Jesus won't want me any more. Maybe I won't get to heaven."

287

His mother said, "Son, you can't hold on to Jesus by yourself. But Jesus can hold on to you. He promised to do that." This made Jimmy glad.

Jesus said to those who are His children and follow His voice, "No one can snatch you out of God's hand." Just as the mother held the little girl, God holds us because we trust in Jesus to save us.

When God holds us, we can be sure we'll go to heaven. When we're sure, we feel safe and happy.

Questions to talk about: Why was Carol holding on to her mother? Why was Carol safe? What did Jimmy worry about? What did his mother tell him? What did Jesus say in our Bible verse for today? Who keeps us close to God in His loving arms?

Bible reading for good readers: John 10:27-30.

Let us pray: Dear Father in heaven, we are so very glad that You are holding us. Please keep us close to You until we reach the shores of heaven, through Jesus Christ, our Savior. Amen.